CHOICES MADE

PRICES PAID

MY STORY

JOHN B. MCINTYRE

BOOK PUBLISHERS NETWORK
Changing the World One Book at a Time

Book Publishers Network
P.O. Box 2256
Bothell • WA • 98041
Ph • 425-483-3040
www.bookpublishersnetwork.com

10 9 8 7 6 5 4 3 2 1

LCCN 2013915740
ISBN 978-1-940598-01-7

Editor: Barbara Kindness
Cover designer: Laura Zugzda
Typographer: Marsha Slomowitz

This is a true story.
The names have been changed to protect the innocent—and the guilty.

A portion of the net proceeds from this book will be donated to at-risk youth programs of the author's choosing.

DEDICATION

This book is dedicated to all the parents who have and are still walking through the despair of drug and alcohol abuse with a difficult child, yet maintain the strength through love to stand firm.

ACKNOWLEDGEMENTS

I would like to thank my publisher and editor for their encouragement in the writing of my story.

I would also like to send a heartfelt thank you to my two sons and parents whose love, hope and faith in me have carried me through the long journey to becoming a productive member of society.

And last but not least to Judie, a very special thanks for challenging me to dream big and aim for the stars.

—JOHNNY

INTRODUCTION

This is a true story that begins with a guy approaching puberty in a middle-class neighborhood in America. It could be in any small-town American city. The hub "village" featured small shops, a theater, a bowling alley, a soda fountain all adjacent to a sports complex of ball diamonds, tennis courts and a gymnasium. Surrounded by well-kept homes with manicured lawns and relatively new schools, this was a neighborhood within a metropolitan city, not suburbia. His family provided for his every need. What more could a kid ask for?

But things then go awry and the story chronicles the journey the young man made and the price he paid for the many poor decisions along the way. From a troubled, out-of-control teen to combat military service to an unwillingness to follow "by the rules" in civilian life, the downward spiral continued: The loss of jobs as a result of a self-induced arrogance probably brought on by drug and alcohol abuse; the failure of two marriages; and ultimately a five-year prison sentence.

Prison finally served as a wake-up call. What kind of effect was his life going to have on his two sons? With the label "convicted felon," how was he going to find work or a place to live?

Determined to be "the best damn dad" in the world and to rebuild his life without drugs, he found the upward climb back into society much slower, more painstaking and frustrating than his fast-paced wayward trek toward destruction.

The countless doors slammed in his face as he attempted to become a normal citizen would probably have caused a lesser man to succumb to his prior life in the drug world. But, he has risen above those temptations and he continues to struggle to become self-sufficient, thanks to an upbeat attitude, a supportive family, and helpful friends.

This is the true story of my son. I hope the telling of it will help other families facing similar challenges.

PROLOGUE

The year was 1975. The Disco Era was in full swing. I was in seventh grade and I was full of energy and ambition. My days were filled with basketball games with my brother Trevor in the alley behind our house, building model cars, and searching for my identity.

We lived in Magnolia, a fairly upscale residential community a few miles northwest of downtown Seattle. It was a quaint little suburb with plenty of activities for kids: a bowling alley, movie theatre, ice cream parlor and a playfield with baseball diamonds, tennis courts, and a full array of jungle gym equipment.

Within just a couple of years after we moved there, everything changed. The ice cream parlor and movie theatre both shut down and became banks. The bowling alley was turned into a liquor store. Nearly every day, the playfield was filled with adult softball leagues, adult flag football, and other activities that didn't include me. My days went from being filled with bowling, movies and ice cream, to aimless wandering around the neighborhood trying to find things to do.

Dad was a Seattle police officer, so being the son of a policeman presented its own set of problems. Some of the kids at my school would call me names like "pigpen," for example. The police in this era were often referred to as pigs or hogs, so names like this were particularly hurtful. I defended my dad's career for a long time and got into a lot of fights for that reason; but before long I started to resent anyone in uniform, or anyone with authority. Defying the rules seemed to be the obvious route to take.

This was the first "fork in the road" of my life: Smoking weed, drinking beer, and avoiding responsibility? Or follow the healthy path of sports, studying, getting good grades, and following "the rules"? The choice was mine. Everybody who knows me—and now you, the reader—will see how and why I made the wrong turn. Not just once but many times—and the prices I paid and continue to pay every day of my life.

This is the beginning of my story.

PART
ONE

CHAPTER 1

It was the summer of 1975. I had a small circle of close friends that I spent most of my time with: Mickey, Danny, Jordan and Carl. We smoked cigarettes, stole booze and beer from our parents' houses, and bought weed from the local "stoner." His name was Larry and, like my brother, he was a year older than I was. They were both in eighth grade at the time.

My friends and I would meet up on the Magnolia Bluff, cutting a trail through the blackberry bushes. We opened up a little hidden area about thirty feet in and brought folding chairs so we could smoke and drink in private. We smoked almost daily for several weeks. It seemed liked I was always stoned. Afterwards, I always went home and straight to my room, pretending I wanted to work on my car models, so Mom didn't suspect anything until one little unfortunate incident.

You see, it didn't take long for the little bit of money we each had to be gone. When you smoke weed and run out of money, what do you do? You have to get creative! So I thought about it for a while, and then had what I thought was a brilliant idea. I knew the "stoner" guy, Larry, always had money and he always had weed. So I talked my brother into convincing Larry to help me out. After a few days and some "negotiations," Larry decided to trust me. I got him to front a half-pound for me. My plan was to sell most of it, leaving a little bit for myself. I was on my way to earning some money and getting a decent-sized stash for my personal use. I went to his house to pick up the half pound. He greeted me at the door and we went inside. Even at thirteen, Larry was a big, strong guy, and his last words to me were, "Don't even think about ripping me off!" I took the warning to heart. I took the weed and stashed it in the bottom of my backpack, and headed home.

I only had a few minutes to hide the bag before going out to do my paper route. I stashed it under my bed and left the house. When I returned home my plan was to find a better hiding spot for the bag. I ran into my bedroom and reached under the bed to retrieve the weed. Shit!

It wasn't there! Panicky, and thinking Trevor had found it and took it to play a joke on me, I headed for his bedroom to get it back.

When I passed the dining room, there it was on the dining room table! My mom was sitting on the couch in the living room with a disgusted look on her face. All she said was, "Wait until your dad gets home!"

That was the longest, scariest hour of my life. My stomach was in knots as I awaited Dad's arrival. Dad got home from work and of course the lecture began, "How could you do this? What were you thinking? Do you realize this stunt could cost me my career with the SPD?"

I tried lying by first telling him that I had found it. Then I told him I was holding it for a friend and I would NEVER use marijuana! The whole time this encounter was going on all I could think about was "HOW AM I GONNA PAY LARRY THE $250 FOR THIS WEED?!"

I found out later that our family basset hound Ernie had discovered the package under my bed and had dragged it out of the bedroom with it in his mouth. Damn dog wouldn't ever fetch a ball or a stick!

I spent the next three weeks of my summer vacation grounded and making up lies to get out of the house—I lied about working, about going to the library, whatever I could think of to get out of the house. Luckily, no one checked up on me or where I was going. The exhilaration and adrenaline rush I got from this was amazing. As soon as I was "free" I decided I would get some pot seeds and try my hand at growing weed so I could make good on my debt to the weed dealer. With absolutely no knowledge or experience growing anything, I failed miserably. The damn plants just would not grow no matter how hard I tried.

I hated going to the library, because that was a breeding ground for the nerds, and I wasn't about to become one of those guys, but I had to figure out how to get these damn plants to grow. I spent a few hours, which seemed like days, reading up on growing vegetables and flowers. I found out that the seed needed to be germinated prior to being placed in the potting soil. I ran to our little spot in the blackberry bush "fort" and proceeded to wet paper towels and gently lay the seeds out. Over the next few days I would get up early and run up to the fort, wet the paper towels and watch my little seeds slowly sprout. I planted them in some good potting soil I stole from mom's garden.

After three weeks of daily interaction with my plants, they grew to a whopping height of about four inches. Harvest time? Oh yeah, I picked all the leaves off the tiny plants and laid them out in the hot August sun waiting for them to dry out enough to roll them up and smoke my harvest. The following afternoon I went up and crumpled up those little leaves and rolled them up and smoked them. It was the worst thing I ever tasted and to make matters worse, I didn't even get a buzz. What went wrong? I never did figure it out. There had to be an easier way.

CHAPTER 2

The fall of 1975 school year began and I found myself lacking the basic tools needed to learn. All I could think about was all that time I wasted in the library to no avail. Learning anything at all seemed pointless. The first few weeks of school were uneventful until mid-October. That was when I heard through the grapevine that there was a really cool drug that got you really high and the best part was that it was free!

Magic mushrooms! I was instantly interested in this. Once again I put my pride aside and headed to the library. I had to get some information about this wonderful mind-altering substance. After two grueling hours of looking up many references on plants and flowers, I found what I was looking for—mushrooms and fungi.

I learned that there were a few varieties of mushrooms that would give a psychedelic high, similar to LSD. Liberty caps and blue ringers were the most common. They grow in the fall and spring, thriving in the morning dew. Cow pastures and fields near bodies of water were the best places to find them.

Living in Magnolia, I knew there wasn't a cow pasture within a million miles (or so it seemed) but I knew of a big field of grass on a hillside right next to the Ballard Locks (the mechanically regulated "doors" that separated Puget Sound from Lake Washington). That was all the information I needed. I got on my bicycle and headed for that field. Arriving at the locks, I saw a plethora of the little psychedelic "shrooms" that were going to be the objects of my latest endeavor. I could hardly contain my excitement!

I got on my bike and headed for school, the entire ride consumed by planning for the task I was ready to embark on tomorrow. All I could think about during the endless hours of that boring ritual we call school was how many mushrooms I saw in the field of grass next to the Ballard Locks. I was mathematically calculating the massive amount of money I was gonna make picking and selling them to my classmates at ten bucks an ounce.

Once again, I was anticipating being the mushroom cartel in the Queen Anne/Magnolia area. Early the following morning I took off long before the school day started. I hauled ass to the locks to harvest my new found wealth, never giving it a thought that if I accidentally picked the wrong kind of mushroom it could be a disaster to the health of my "customers."

Once I got to the locks I picked and picked mushrooms, filling a few kitchen garbage bags with the "organic gold," totally losing track of time. I picked and bagged my crop for over two hours, well into the first two periods of my school day. But who could blame me for missing a few hours of the time I would be wasting in school anyway. After all, I no longer needed school because I was well on my way to becoming rich selling fungi for profit—lots of profit!

Having to maintain a somewhat normal image, I stashed the organic gold in some bushes and headed to school. When I arrived, I was sent directly to the principal's office.

I received an attendance letter that was to be taken home, signed by my parents and returned the next day. *Shit! How was I gonna explain to my mom and dad that I was three hours late for school, after mom watched me leave the house an hour before school started?*

It was time to master the art of manipulation and deception. In other words, lying through my teeth. After what seemed like the longest day of my life, the final school bell rang and I ran to my locked bicycle. I peddled as fast as I could until my legs burned, heading to the locks to pick up my stash of mushrooms.

When I arrived, I discovered they were gone! I had wasted all that time picking those mushrooms only to find that the park maintenance guys during the course of the day must've thrown my bags of mushrooms away.

Dammit! I thought. After all that work picking those things and bagging them into kitchen trash bags and stashing them, it was all for nothing! Dammit! So I headed home dejected and defeated.

The following morning I woke up bright and early, got on my bicycle and headed back to the locks for a second time. Upon arriving, I saw my organic gold everywhere on the field so the excitement took over again and I ran all over picking and bagging my little personal gold mine. I got three kitchen trash bags full and this time I was gonna find a better hiding place.

I decided the best possible place to hide three bags of mushrooms was about ten feet up in a pine tree, so I climbed up and stashed my three bags of gold. I got on my bicycle, headed for school, and got there just in time for first period. After another long day of school and the final bell had rung, I went back to the locks to retrieve my bags. Whew! They were still right where I left them. I climbed up, got the bags, jumped down, and went back behind the building to divide them up into one-ounce baggies.

I stuffed them in my backpack and headed for home. After dinner, I called my friends and we agreed to meet down at the park to play Frisbee and football. I gave each of them a baggie and we ate mushrooms and proceeded to lazily throw the football until the full effects of the mushrooms made us oblivious to our surroundings.

At the peak of our high, we started throwing the Frisbee back and forth because it looked really cool going through the air. After about ten minutes, Mickey climbed up on a scaffolding that had been hung by painters working on the side of a building. He hollered down at us: "Hey, guys, should I jump?"

"No, not a good idea," I replied. "Come on back down."

We finally all convinced him it probably wasn't a real good idea, and he climbed down. Back to Frisbee tossing, Danny ran across the field to catch a Frisbee that wasn't really there. He ran into the backstop of the baseball diamond. While he lay there stunned, the rest of us just laughed and laughed. Thankfully he only got a couple of cuts and bruises.

The next day, Danny, Mickey, Jordan and I quickly spread the word about this wonderful high we had just experienced the night before. My heart just sank when it seemed like nobody was interested in experiencing this euphoria.

So it was back to the drawing board for me. My idea of making a whole bunch of quick cash had been another miserable failure. Winter was arriving. It was getting colder and soon Christmas was right around the corner. I spent the next few months hanging out on street corners smoking weed and cigarettes.

CHAPTER 3

I spent the following summer of 1976 doing nothing more than avoiding the garden and household chores my mom and dad would ask me to do. Dad asked me to dig a hole…I broke a shovel. Mom asked me to weed the flower bed…I pulled all the flowers and all the pretty things that she had planted, and of course did my best to leave all the weeds intact and growing.

In the evening, I would go to my room and open up my bedroom window and smoke countless cigarettes, tossing the butts out the window which, of course, Mom would find. My story would always be that somebody was setting me up. I never could sneak out the window because it wouldn't open more than five inches, so escape was out of the question.

I realized toward the end of summer that smoking weed was something I did not enjoy, but I continued doing it anyway because that was the thing to do among all my friends. My sole purpose of that summer was to fit in with the cool crowd, and the cool crowd were weed smokers.

Near the end of August it was time to get ready for school again—the beginning of eighth grade. My mind was swirling with ideas on how to prepare for the unending lies and constant attempts to manipulate the system. Well, I had a pretty close call that should have changed me right then. I was wandering around at a street fair in Magnolia Village when my brother caught up with me and asked if I wanted to go camping with Grandma and Grandpa. Of course, I did. So I got on my bicycle and rode uphill as fast as I could to get home to pack my stuff. I crossed 34th Avenue without looking either way. I was struck by a car and thrown from my bike. Mom was watching from our living room window and saw my body as it went flying through the air. Frantic, she ran down the three blocks to 34th. An aid car arrived and the paramedic wrapped my leg and examined for broken bones. Luckily, there were none! Ironically, the driver of the car that hit me, which was one hundred percent my fault, was the guy AAA hired to go from school to school to teach kids about bicycle safety! Guess I didn't learn too much.

I found myself feeling pretty cocky in September when the school year began because I was no longer a puny seventh-grader. I was a big bad eighth-grader now; not quite as cool as the ninth-graders, but now I had some little seventh-graders I could pick on. But during the entire time I was bullying the seventh-graders and trying to fit in with my new classmates while avoiding the ninth-graders, I was going through puberty and trying to make a name for myself among my classmates. So *anybody* who transferred into our junior high was a target for me—especially if they were smaller or appeared to be weak.

Well, there was a new kid in school by the name of Andy and he looked like a perfect target for me to bully. That turned out to be a very large mistake on my part. What I didn't know at the time was his father was a pro boxer and had taught his son how to fight. Every time I saw him in the hallway, I would dump his books out of his hand and call him names; just boldly pick on him at every opportunity. Finally, about mid-November, he had had enough of my bullying and decided he wanted to fight me in the park after school. So I, being the big tough guy that I thought I was, told everybody I knew that I was going to kick this guy's ass at three o'clock in the park.

"Come on down by the swings and watch the fun," I boasted. All my friends and classmates followed me down to the park, excited to see the action.

Andy was waiting there for my arrival. I'm not quite sure but I think he hit me about fourteen times before I could blink an eye. Very embarrassed and slightly woozy, I put my hand out and asked him to be my friend. Andy and I remained friends for the rest of his time at that school.

In early December, I was with my friends Eddie and Matt and the three of us decided we were going to steal some booze from my parents' basement, from Matt's house and Eddie's house. So on a late Thursday night, while my parents were sleeping, I snuck into the basement, took several bottles of booze, and filled small club soda bottles with the assortment of liquors that were in the liquor cabinet. I took my little bottles to school in a backpack and met up with Eddie and

Matt after school. The three of us headed over to Eddie's house. The liquor tasted terrible but we kept drinking it anyway until we were all totally bombed.

When it was time to head home, I stumbled my way to my house. Both of my parents were at work, and during the school week my brother Trevor and I had our own set of chores to complete before Mom got home. This particular week my main chore for the day was to load the dishwasher. When I staggered through the back door, my brother was loading the dishwasher and he was already livid. When he saw my condition, he became even more pissed off, because I was so drunk I could barely stand up, let alone utter a coherent sentence. To make things even worse, I was giggling when I stumbled into the kitchen. Trevor tried his very best to stuff my entire body inside the dishwasher, and I didn't even care because I was so drunk.

Then, he felt bad, I guess, because what he ended up doing was carrying me to bed, pulling the covers up over me, and walking out, closing the door behind him. Later on, when Mom got home from work and asked Trevor where I was, bless his heart he told her I was sick and in bed sleeping. I spent the rest of the night passed out.

I woke up the next morning feeling worse than I had ever felt in my life. This was my first experience of a hangover. All I could think of was how to make the pain go away, the nasty taste in my mouth, and—my God!—was my head ever pounding hard! Now, while eavesdropping on some of my parents' conversations and, of course, from watching TV, I had heard that the best cure for a hangover was a drink, "the hair of the dog that bit you!"

You guessed it! I snuck back downstairs and had a big swig of some crème de menthe. That was the only liquor I could stand the smell of at that time. Nothing immediately good came of that decision. I ran to the bathroom and vomited for a solid ten minutes. So the crème de menthe didn't work for the hangover, but after I got done "driving the porcelain bus," I felt so much better.

After school one day, when it was my week to do the vacuuming, Trevor and I got home at pretty much the same time. It seemed most days there was always something that caused some sort of a fight with him. This time it was the vacuum. He was listening to a record while he was loading the dishwasher, and the record player was in the living room. I turned the vacuum on and began my chore. Trevor came out of the kitchen. "Hey, Johnny, could you wait until this song is over?"

"Oh, go to hell," I said, and the fight was on! I slammed the vacuum cleaner into the table that the record player was on, causing the record to scratch. This was a Kirby brand vacuum cleaner, which was said to be indestructible, but as we were wrestling and fighting throughout the living room, Trevor got his hands on the vacuum cleaner and hit me over the head with the handle—so hard that the handle folded in half, gave me a hell of a headache, and broke the unbreakable vacuum cleaner. I don't know how it happened but somehow I got blamed for all this and was placed on restriction for a week, plus I didn't get my allowance.

My brother and I fought all the time, which drove Mom crazy, but that didn't stop us. We had a real love/hate relationship. The funny thing was that even if we fought all the time and beat the crap out of each other every minute of every day, nobody else had better mess with my brother; we always had each other's back, no matter what.

For the next couple of weeks, I spent a lot of time stealing liquor and going over to Eddie's and drinking booze with him, but I had learned my lesson quickly not to drink so much so fast, therefore avoiding that terrible feeling of the morning after.

I looked forward to mid-December when it was time for Christmas vacation from school. During the first four days of Christmas break, my grandpa Doug took me up to the mountains for elk hunting. Any time I got to spend time with Grandpa Doug was always really fun because Grandpa seemed to understand me and he was my hero. Not only did I love being with him, I really loved getting out in the woods with a gun and tramping around looking for any sign of elk. Those days that I spent in the woods with Grandpa were better than any experience I had had with any mind-altering substance.

We got back to Seattle three days before Christmas. I remember that Christmas more vividly than any other in my life because I got a cool new ski jacket and a ski hat and gloves. I loved skiing as much as I loved hunting. I lived in that ski hat for the next several weeks.

New Year's Eve came and went and then it was time to get back to school. Well, I continued to wear that ski hat every day all day, until my algebra teacher, Mr. Smith, kicked me out of class because I refused to take it off. I got sent to the principal's office and verbally reprimanded for not listening to my teacher and removing my hat upon his request. This made me hate school even more.

After the terrible demeaning visit to the principal's office, I decided it was time to have another drinking escapade with Eddie and Matt. So I tracked them down after class and we set it up for the next day. It was off to Dad's liquor cabinet once again! When I got home that afternoon, I realized that the booze supply in the basement had obviously been tampered with, so I, in my infinite wisdom, decided that pouring tap water into the bottles would take them back up to the level they were when I first started stealing the booze. Wow! What a great idea; I felt like a rocket scientist.

The following day, my friends and I went to Eddie's house and proceeded to get drunk. Practicing moderation didn't work that time and I found myself totally smashed again. I stumbled home again but managed to fake my way through my chores, brush my teeth and wash my face to hide the fact that I was out of it. I think it worked because nobody said anything.

I pretended to go do my homework in my bedroom, smoked a couple of cigarettes out the back window, and took a nap until dinner. When Mom called that dinner was ready I kind of stumbled in and sat down to eat. They probably thought I was still groggy from my nap. During the meal, Dad announced that we were going skiing at Snoqualmie Summit on Friday and Saturday of that week. I was so excited!

Right after dinner, I raced to my room and started packing all my ski gear, only to find that my ski hat was missing! I paced the floor trying to figure out where the hell my ski hat was. Then it came to me. I must've left it at Eddie's house during our little drinking escapade. So I went to the living room and told my mom that I left my ski hat at Eddie's. Mom didn't like Eddie as she considered him a bad apple, and it seemed like I gravitated toward bad apples. So she told me in a stern voice to get my ass down to Eddie's tomorrow right after school and get my hat because we were leaving that night for the Summit.

Eddie wasn't in school that day and neither was Matt so I skipped my last two classes and headed over to Eddie's house, hoping and praying he would be home. I went into the garage and knocked on the basement door.

Eddie hollered down, "Who is it?"

I replied, "It's Johnny. I need my ski hat."

"Wait a minute," Eddie said, so I did.

Five minutes went by so I knocked again. "Eddie, I need my hat."

Again he replied "Just a minute, Johnny."

Finally, after what seemed to be an eternity, he told me to come up. I went into the house and started to climb the stairs and when I was about five stairs from the top, an upstairs door opened, Eddie reached around the corner, grabbed a .22 caliber rifle, pointed it at me, and fired!

I fell backwards down the stairs, and all Eddie could say was, "Aw, c'mon. It wasn't loaded. Quit faking it."

I reached inside my jacket and pulled out a bloody hand! Both Eddie and Matt freaked out more than I did. Dazed, I went up the stairs to the kitchen to unzip my jacket only to find that my shirt was bloody. Both guys were totally pale, almost started hyperventilating, and went into a panic. I just watched the blood oozing out, kind of mesmerized by this hole in my chest (I believe that would be shock!). Eddie got a washcloth and some ice and put it over that spot.

My mom was working down at J&J Pharmacy seven blocks away so I figured I should give her a call. Eddie begged me to lie to her so he wouldn't get in trouble for shooting me. So I called Mom at work and proceeded to tell her that I had been hit by sniper fire while I was walking down McGraw Street. Mom told me to come down to the pharmacy and let her take a look. She obviously thought I had been hit by a BB from a long way away so she didn't appear too concerned. I put an ice pack over the wound and walked the seven blocks to her work. By the time I got to the pharmacy, there was quite a bit of blood on me. Mom took one look at me and absolutely panicked! There was just one other person in the store right then, a little old man, so she begged him to give me a ride to the chiropractor on 34th, the only doctor still around in Magnolia at that hour.

I got in this man's car—I think it was about a 1946 Plymouth that had springs sticking out through the cushions of the front seat. All I could think of at that time was a Goofy cartoon where the characters were driving the old Model A convertibles with springs sticking through the seats. It was pretty laughable. The man got me to the chiropractor who immediately put me on one of his adjustment tables and stuck a flexible probe in the hole in my chest.

Mom arrived almost immediately only to have the chiropractor tell her to "just put a Band-Aid on it. The slug will work its way to the surface of John's skin, then you can take a razor blade to cut the skin and take it out."

Mom replied, "I think I'll take my son to Ballard hospital!"

When we arrived at the hospital, they immediately started prepping me for surgery. They had just finished giving me an anesthetic and were wheeling me down the corridor towards the operating room when my dad showed up in his Seattle police uniform! He walked alongside the gurney, asking me how I was feeling. I was a bit woozy because the anesthetic was just taking effect. His next question took me by surprise. "Eddie shot you, didn't he?"

All I could think of was *How the hell does he know that?*

My reply was, "Huh? How did you know that?"

"I'm a police officer, it's my job." And right then my father's career earned my undeniable respect. My dad really knew his job and he was very good at it. When I came out of surgery, Dr. Gonzalez, the surgeon who performed the operation, came into post-op as I was coming to. In a serious tone, he said, "Young man, God must have something very special planned for you because that slug made multiple passes through your insides and never hit a vital organ."

I was sent home four days later to recover. Kids from my class brought my homework to our house to keep me from falling too far behind. I returned to school two weeks later. Another close call.

On my first day back, between second and third periods, a ninth-grader came up behind me and gave me a shove. Eddie saw him and proceeded to beat the crap out of him and told him he'd better never lay a hand on me again. He pretty much made himself my guardian/protector from then on. I became the center of attention at my junior high, because I was probably the first student in the history of that school to have been shot. The next three months were pretty uneventful for the most part. I still drank a lot of beer and smoked weed with my friends but that was about it.

At the end of eighth grade, I began my summer with Mom and Dad dropping the big bomb on me: I wasn't going back to that junior high in the fall. I was going to a Catholic all-boys high school on Capitol Hill. Oh, my God! This was the worst news I'd ever received. *Why would my parents do this to me?* was all I could think. Everything I knew was at public school, and I hated the fact that Mom and Dad were gonna take me out of my comfort zone. What did I do to deserve this shit? I was going to be the top dog, a ninth-grader, at my junior high next year. My mom and dad wanted to take everything I enjoyed away from me, and that pissed me off; made me feel like my parents were really trying hard to make my life unbearable, and they were succeeding. Needless to say, that summer was spent drunk or high every single day.

CHAPTER 4

That fall, my brother, my new friend Randy, and I all caught the bus together on the first day of school. Oh, my God, I was a freshman, the lowest of the low and all my friends were halfway across the city. I spent the first two weeks of school really resenting my parents. I couldn't be a rebel without a cause. I believed I was a rebel with a cause—a major cause. After all, it wasn't my fault. I didn't ask to be transferred to this all boys' Catholic high school.

I decided I was going to cause as much trouble as possible and see exactly what I could get away with. I became argumentative, disruptive; in fact, I was a complete asshole. I found myself in the principal's office almost on a daily basis. Aside from that, the schoolwork was challenging, which was something I'd never experienced in public school, so I inadvertently found that I was applying myself and actually learning. This was not my intention at all. I felt my rebellious mentality starting to fade, so in order to keep that rebel attitude, I forced myself to create problems.

A couple of examples of what I did to create mayhem: I would go to a local department store in downtown Seattle and steal cassette tapes. I would go to the local five-and-dime in Magnolia and steal anything that wasn't glued down. It wasn't long before I got caught. Finally, happily, I was back in a bad light (after all, this was where I felt most comfortable). I spent the next couple of weeks grounded, but that wasn't very effective punishment because I had two free hours between the end of the school day and arriving home. Needless to say, I had plenty of time to cause plenty of trouble so in that two hours I continued stealing cassette tapes nearly every day. And, of course, there was time to be smoking plenty of weed.

As the school year progressed, I found that I was doing extremely well in every subject with the exception of French. Since I was not very interested in learning some stupid foreign language, I didn't even attempt to complete a single assignment, not realizing—until later in the semester—that this was a graduation requirement. When I found out I needed to pass this class in order to complete my education, I did the bare minimum and eventually did pass this class. (I think I may know six words in French.)

Randy and I became very good friends and spent a lot of time together. We started working with the basketball coaches and became trainers. This was actually pretty fun, and it kept me out of the house most every afternoon. Traveling all over the state with the team was a great experience. But I still had my dirty little secret that I never told anybody from that school—I was a pothead. I never even let Randy know. By the end of the school year I had managed to keep myself off of restriction.

The spring dance at Queen Anne High was something I was not going to miss. Mickey, Danny, Carl and Jordan all planned this evening of smoking weed, drinking booze, and causing trouble. For the first time in a long time, I was allowed to go to the dance without resorting to any lies or deceit, so I left our house in Magnolia to go to the bus stop and catch the three buses that would take me to Queen Anne High School.

When I got to the base of Queen Anne hill waiting for my third transfer, I decided to hell with it and started hitchhiking. After about twenty minutes, a little dark green Volkswagen Dasher pulled over and picked me up. The driver obviously had been tipping a few drinks. We drove through the back streets of Queen Anne and down one narrow residential street where the guy sideswiped four cars. To my amazement, he started laughing about it.

I said, "Man, you just wrecked your car!"

"Ain't my car," he said. "I stole it!"

So, of course, I wanted to take a turn behind the wheel. He pulled over and got out and we traded seats. I started driving and this was where I belonged, behind the wheel of a stolen car. I drove around for about an hour. Seeing how much fun I was having driving this car, the guy asked me if I wanted it.

"Sure, I do," I said.

Then he said, "The only rule is that you have to ditch it by Sunday night 'cause the owner is going to be home on Monday."

I didn't pay any attention to what he said. I just wanted to drive!

I parked the little Dasher about a block away from our house, up on 36th Avenue, and Saturday and Sunday drove all over town. Nowhere to go, nowhere to be. I just drove and drove. Sunday night was the night I was supposed to unload the car, but I was having so much fun with it that I thought I could push the envelope and drive it for just a few more days.

Monday morning came and I had a decision to make: Should I catch the bus to school? Or should I drive my car? Everybody who knows me knows the answer to that question. Of course I drove the car! I drove back and forth to school that whole week.

On Friday I decided it was time to ditch the car. I drove to school and at the end of the day I headed over to Eddie's house to have him and/or Matt follow me down to Beach Road where I would dump the car. Matt showed up about ten minutes later, and they decided they wanted to strip the stereo and the seats out of the Dasher. So we broke out the tools and proceeded to take apart the interior.

Once the seats were out, where was I supposed to sit to drive the car? So, we loosened all the bolts but left the driver's seat intact. Matt asked if he could take the car out for a spin. I didn't care so I gave him the key, and off he went, returning about forty-five minutes later. We removed the driver's seat, set a milk crate in its place, and arranged for me to go down to Beach Road, park the car, and wait for Matt and Eddie to show up to give me a ride out of there.

Since he was a police officer in the city of Seattle, my dad obviously knew a lot of policemen, as did I. While I was sitting in the car on Beach Road waiting for my friends, a Seattle police car pulled up and one of my dad's fellow-officers pulled up behind the Dasher. I got out of the car and waved to Officer Bailey. He got out too and said, "Hi Johnny, whose car is this?"

"Oh, it's my Uncle Bill's."

"Your uncle drives a Ford Fairmont, Johnny. Now, you want to tell me whose car this is?"

I found myself in a holding cell at the Seattle Police Department. I sat there for approximately two hours, figuring I would rather rot in jail than face my father, since everyone there knew who I was. I was so embarrassed!

Three hours later, reality set in. I started bawling and begging the officer on duty to call my dad to get me out of this mess I had gotten myself into. Dad showed up angry and obviously embarrassed at the fact that he was a police officer and his son had just been arrested for stealing a car. They released me to his custody. I hung my head in shame as we walked out to his car and the drive home was eerily silent. We got home and not a word was spoken until he finally said, "I don't even want to look at you. Get out of my living room!"

So I went to my bedroom, closed the door, and lay down. I don't think Dad said two words to me for the next three months. You could cut the tension in our house with a knife. Even to this day, nobody believes that I did not actually steal that car!

The end of the school year and pretty much all that summer there was not very much communication between my father and myself. I had a paper route all summer, which essentially was my first real paying job. I saved some money and decided that I was going to get some tropical fish so I got a twenty-nine gallon fish tank and all the filters, heaters and decorative stuff to go inside the tank.

I went downtown to the fish store on First Avenue and bought two Oscars. I spent the next couple of months going to the fish store every day after school and made friends with a guy by the name of Dave, who was the fish expert at that store. With my weed habit and my drinking habit, I didn't have very much money. Dave would make me a deal on some fish if I could bring him stuff, like tools and jewelry. So over the next month and a half, I stole a bunch of little stuff to trade for fish supplies.

I really wanted this fifty-five gallon tank and Dave told me that I had to get some more expensive stuff if I wanted that tank so I stole a pair of diamond earrings from my mom, and a chainsaw from my dad's garage, took them down to the fish store and Dave said that he would pack up the fish tank for me the following day. The next day I went to the fish store to get my fish tank and the lady at the front counter informed me that Dave had quit the night before. Seriously? This was my first experience in learning how shady the world of crime is. The chainsaw was gone, the earrings were gone, and I got nothing for them.

Fall turned into winter and after Christmas break I went back to school. I no longer had to take the bus because Randy had gotten his license and would drive me to school every day. So I didn't have a whole lot of time between school and home to get into any mischief, but I still managed.

On April 4, the eve of my sixteenth birthday, I got home that evening and Dad was waiting for me, the angriest I'd ever seen him. He asked me where his revolver was. For once I was not guilty, so I told him I had no idea where his gun went.

"You have twenty-four hours to come up with my gun or you can get the hell out of my house," he shouted.

I couldn't help him with the gun dilemma because I had nothing to do with it. So I figured the best move for me would be to go elsewhere to live. I packed up a few things, said goodbye to my fish, and left. Hell of a way to spend my sixteenth birthday!

I went to stay with some friends. Almost a week went by and my brother tracked me down to tell me that Dad found the gun and wanted me to come home. Evidently he had changed hiding places for fear that I would get my hands on it and forgot where he put it. Honestly, I don't blame him. I would have done the same thing as a parent.

My friend Jeremy and I often went out partying with another friend, Ronnie. Jeremy had a 1961 Chevy Biscayne station wagon that we used whenever we wanted to go out drinking, He was a crazy driver. One night we went up to Fort Lawton, into the park to drink. We had no idea the park closed at dusk. We drank until approximately eleven p.m. and when we decided to leave we discovered they had locked the gates and we couldn't get out. Jeremy, in his infinite wisdom, decided to ram the gate, thinking it was the only way we were going to escape.

No way were Ronnie and I about to stay in the car, so we got out and walked across the street to watch the show. Jeremy backed up as far as he could and floored it, hitting the gate at about thirty miles an hour. It didn't come down so he hit it ten or eleven more times to no avail. It wasn't long before the police showed up so Ronnie and I took off. The car was totaled and Jeremy went to jail.

A month later, Jeremy and I were out partying again, this time in a '71 Torino. Driving down Government Way at about a hundred miles an hour, he suddenly came upon a car in front of us doing about twenty-five. Jeremy decided to pass it on the right—thread the needle between it and a truck parked against the curb. This did not work out very well! He sideswiped the truck and literally destroyed the whole passenger side of his car, shattering the glass on my side window. I received a glass shard shower, thinking it was the end for me.

We were both so paranoid about getting caught there that he sped into the alley behind his mom's house, removed the front fender and the door and buried them in his backyard. I wonder if that fender and door are still buried behind that house.

For the remainder of the school year, my home life seemed extremely calm and rational. Don't get me wrong. I still got my weed smoking in and my occasional theft of booze from Dad's liquor cabinet. Whenever I spent time at my friends' houses we were usually trying to figure out better ways to make bongs, were eating mushrooms, drinking booze, and smoking weed.

Soon after school was out, Mom and Dad went on a vacation and left my brother in charge of the house. Three days after their departure he had a party, and I came home from my friend Mickey's house to find about fifteen people downstairs playing pool. When I walked down the stairs and walked through the door into the rec room, the first thing I saw was a small pile of white powdery substance on a mirror. Two people immediately stepped in front of it to hide it from my field of vision. I looked at my brother and asked if I could try it.

"Hell no, you little asshole," he answered. "This shit's expensive."

I knew it was cocaine, and all I could think about was how to convince Trevor to let me try this drug I'd heard so much about. So I threatened to tell Mom and Dad if he would not let me try some. That naturally pissed him off and he called me every name in the book, but then he decided it was in his best interest to go ahead and let me try it.

He drew me up a little line and handed me the straw. I took it, bent over, and snorted my line. Wow! My whole face went numb! This was the first time I had ever experienced something so amazing. My heart felt like it was going to jump out of my chest, my face was numb, and my mind was running a million miles a second! This was by far the best feeling I had ever experienced.

Ten minutes later, all I could think about was doing it again. I went back in there to convince my brother to give me another line. After a couple more threats and a pretty huge argument, he gave in and gave me another one. The feeling was still pretty amazing but nowhere near as good as the first one. I spent the next couple of days trying to figure out how I could make money so I could buy some of that white powdery substance for myself. I think they call it chasing the Dragon.

So, I started experimenting with different things that could earn me some quick cash. I had heard about smoking parsley and other green spices, and people buying parsley thinking it was marijuana. So I spent a couple of hours in our kitchen trying to figure out what I could roll into a joint and sell to my schoolmates. After about twenty minutes of thinking and searching, I grabbed rolling paper and a teabag. I emptied the tea out of the teabag into the paper, rolled it up, and went out to the back porch and sparked it up.

Oh, my God, this shit smelled just like marijuana when you burned it. So I grabbed the whole box of Red Rose tea, removed the tea from all the bags, and rolled them into multiple joints that I planned on selling for a dollar apiece, so I could earn enough money to buy my cocaine.

As with every other entrepreneurial experiment I tried, this too failed miserably. I sold about twenty joints and had about fifteen people really disgusted because they didn't
get high off of my joints. And to make matters even worse, Mom found a little baggie full of joints in my coat pocket.

The calm, cool nature my home life had become was gone in an instant. I spent the rest of that summer grounded, pulling weeds, and performing general household chores.

CHAPTER 5

There was one big difference to the start of the next school year: I was now an upperclassman, a junior one year away from graduation. I didn't have too many friends in that school and my best friend, Randy, was graduating that year.

I sailed through the first couple of months. My grades were actually better than they had been in the past and once again I found myself kind of getting into the curriculum. I think a lot of that might have been caused by the fact that I really cut down on my marijuana smoking late that previous summer. I still smoked weed with my friends, but nowhere near as often as I had in the past. I think experiencing cocaine and the heart-pounding, chest-thumping euphoria that that brought on soured me on the dull, lifeless high that marijuana provided. I found myself drinking a lot of beer and booze, but avoiding marijuana most of the time.

Many of my friends had gotten cars from their parents, but I knew my driving days were a long way away because I had been such an asshole in the past. That was okay because all my friends had cars.

As autumn turned into winter, my closest friends and I were quickly becoming dependent on alcohol. It seemed like every day was an adventure trying to figure out where we were going to get booze or beer to satisfy that craving. I remember one night in particular we were all pretty buzzed. Mom and Dad weren't home that evening so Mickey and I went down to the basement. In the very back corner of the top shelf of the liquor cabinet was a tall, narrow bottle of Greek brandy called Metaxa. Mickey convinced me that Dad would never miss it so we grabbed it, jumped into another one of my friend's cars, a Volkswagen beetle, and drove off.

Mickey cracked the seal and took a big swig, spat it out the side window, and threw the bottle out the window saying, "That's the worst shit I've ever had. How can your dad drink that shit?" (Thirty-three years later, my dad still remembers that bottle of Metaxa. It was a gift from a very good friend of his who had since passed away.)

In late November, it started snowing like crazy in Seattle, and I was anxious to get up to the mountains and go skiing. I had a job at a burger joint so I was making a little money, and the Alpine Hut ski shop was just three doors away from where I worked.

Leaving work one afternoon, I spotted a red Ferrari parked in front of a warehouse. My curiosity led me to go closer to the car to check it out. It was beautiful, so I peered inside the open driver side window. There, on the center console, lay a money clip. I quickly grabbed it and casually walked away from the car. I waited until I got to a house two blocks away before pulling it out of my pocket and counting the cash. There was over three hundred dollars in that money clip.

Obviously, my next stop was Alpine Hut. I bought gloves, boots, bindings, and a pair of skis. This was my lucky day. I was ready to go skiing. My only dilemma was how I was going to explain to my parents how I acquired enough cash to buy new ski gear. I didn't really care about anything but preparing for what was sure to be the best skiing year ever. Just as I expected, Mom asked where I got the money for the skis, boots and bindings, so it became necessary for me to lie my way through this dilemma. I told her that I got a good paycheck and a bonus for doing a good job—that's how I could afford the skis. It's still hard for me to imagine she would believe the fact that I got a bonus for working because I was so damn lazy around the house.

Every Saturday I took the ski bus up to Snoqualmie Summit with thirty to forty other kids from Magnolia. One of the kids that also caught that bus was Eddie, my friend who had shot me. Eddie, Matt and I skied every week together, although I had been forbidden to maintain a friendship with him after the shooting.

One Saturday in February, the three of us were skiing the trails in an out-of-bounds area, and we were getting a little bit nervous because it was dark and the bus was leaving soon, so we cut down the side of the trail. I got ahead of the other two and Eddie hollered for me to wait for him. I stopped and leaned against a tree, which had about eight feet of snowdrift on it. I fell into a hole eight feet under, headfirst. The two guys frantically dug and dug until they had me freed from my freezing grave. After that the joke was that Eddie had tried to kill me then saved my life. Pretty even trade, huh?

We made it to the bus on time, loaded up our ski gear, and boarded the bus. Luckily the only bad thing that happened was that I lost one ski glove and I was really cold. For the next couple of weeks after I nearly froze to death on the mountain, I found myself focusing a little bit more on studies and being a better person. I had cheated death again and, for about a week, I was thankful to be alive. Then it was back to the same old bad habits—stealing cassette tapes, smoking weed, and drinking. As my junior year progressed I found myself skipping school a lot more often than attending.

Over the next couple of months, I spent every day lying, cheating and stealing my way through life. I found that my trips to the department store to steal cassette tapes was the only activity that gave me that heart-pounding excitement I yearned for, so those trips became more and more frequent.

In April 1980, I turned seventeen and my brother turned eighteen. He was getting ready to graduate, which meant that Randy would be graduating also. That saddened me because my only friend in the school would no longer be there. I had to fill that void somehow, and the only thing I knew was drugs, alcohol, and theft. So the next month of my life was a blur, no holds barred.

At the end of May, as my brother was preparing for his graduation ceremony, I wound up getting caught stealing cassette tapes from The Bon. Everybody in my family was extremely pissed off because I was raining on my brother's parade. In fact, I had become very good at ruining every positive family occasion. I went to court and was ordered to do twenty hours of community service. I didn't have a driver's license or car, so the court made an accommodation for this by assigning me to a nursing home within walking distance of our house.

My first day of community service was scheduled during spring break. Amazingly, I showed up on time and prepared to work with the groundskeeper, Chase. After he introduced himself to me, we walked the grounds together and he gave me the tasks I was supposed to do. By my third four-hour day, Chase and I had become pretty good friends and I made him aware of a lot of my past experiences with drugs and booze.

Suddenly, all my dreams were answered—Chase was a cocaine dealer. He and I went back into the maintenance shed and he proceeded to put out a couple of lines. We snorted them and suddenly community service didn't seem like too much of a punishment. Over the next two days, I went everywhere with Chase to make deliveries and pickups and anything that would keep me in his good graces so he would continue giving me lines.

On my last day of community service, Chase asked me if I wanted to take a ride with him into downtown Seattle. Without even asking why, I said "yes, definitely." We got in the car, took off, and next thing I knew we were at the Four Seasons Hotel, heading up to the penthouse suite. The guitarist for a prominent classic rock band answered the door and waved us in without saying a word. Chase pulled a very large bag of cocaine out of his duffel bag and handed it to the guy. I was speechless because I was in the presence of a great rock 'n roll star.

We sat down and Chase laid out multiple large lines on the glass coffee table. The three of us snorted a lot of cocaine. Dusk set over the city and all three of us were extremely high. Then Chase asked our new friend what his plans were for the evening.

"Our band is giving a concert at the Seattle Center Coliseum at seven-thirty," he replied.

Chase started laughing uncontrollably, looked at his watch and laughed some more. I looked at him wondering what was so funny when I realized it was seven forty-five. So Chase and I were responsible for the delay of a major concert by one of the top bands in the nation!

The guitarist called the limo and invited us to join him. What an opportunity! Hanging out in the penthouse of the Four Seasons Hotel with the world-famous rock star, a ride to the Coliseum in a stretch limo, and sitting backstage with more booze and more cocaine than I had ever seen in one place before. I was in heaven!

At the end of the concert, the limo picked us up and the rest of the band got into another limo and we all went back up to the penthouse. Damn, those guys could party! I was drunk as hell and wired for sound. We partied until the wee hours of the morning.

Chase and I stayed in contact with each other for approximately three to four weeks after that concert. I don't know whether he got busted, killed, or if he just moved. I went to the nursing home a few times after that and his car wasn't in his parking spot. I never did figure out where he went or what happened to him. He just vanished without a trace.

Returning to school after spring break wasn't easy. My brain had been polluted with so much alcohol, coke and weed that even a full week later I was pretty much unable to function normally. Even the simple task of getting my ass out of bed to go to school was almost impossible. But I managed. The rest of the school year was spent hanging out in the parking garage of Cabrini Hospital, which was across the street from O'Dea, smoking weed and drinking with the only two people in that school that I hung out with, Tommy and Val. On the second to last day of school, Val and I drank booze in the parking garage before school and were totally bombed before eight a.m. Was I really going down this road? Only transients and Skid Row bums got drunk that early in the morning!

I stumbled my way to school and during my first class quietly did my best to avoid eye contact and avoid any communication with anyone. Whew, I made it through that class. But my second-period class, algebra trig, was a different story. I never did see eye-to-eye with that teacher. Historically I was always disruptive and confrontational with him. As I walked into the class still drunk, the teacher glared at me, and that pissed me off, but the good news was that Val had that class also, so I thought he would back me up.

Midway through the class, I felt that the teacher was picking on me so I slurred a few choice expletives toward him. He lost his cool. His face was red and the veins were popping out on his forehead. He pointed at the door and told me to get my ass out in the hallway. I left. Gladly. I didn't want to stay in that class anyway. A short time later he came out, and I called him an asshole; the fight was on. He slapped the shit out of me and told me to go directly to the principal's office. I found out later that day that he played semipro hockey; I sure picked the wrong guy to mess with.

I was asked not to return to O'Dea for my senior year. This was a huge victory for me. I finally got what I wanted. Ha ha! I won. This was exactly what I wanted—to graduate with all my true friends from Queen Anne High. Life was golden. But then I realized I would eventually have to face the music when I got home.

I hung out down at Freeway Park and roamed around downtown Seattle for the next four hours. On the one hand, I was extremely happy because I wasn't ever going to have to go back to that school again, but a small part of me was worried about my parents' reaction when I informed them that I would be going to Queen Anne High to finish my education. I stayed downtown long enough to make it look like I had completed the school day.

To my surprise, Brother McGraw (the school principal) had already contacted Mom to inform her that I was not welcome back at that school. So needless to say, the shit hit the fan as soon as I walked through the door. Mom was furious. She told me that she and my dad had worked so hard to put me into a good school and I was throwing it all away. And, as I had heard many times before, the last statement she made was, "You just wait until your dad gets home."

Dad got home later that day, and when he heard about it he basically had nothing to say to me. He told my mom to get me out of his sight; that he didn't even want to look at me. So I went to my room and lay down. The hangover was beginning and the last thing my head needed was to get yelled at. So I looked at this as a victory too. I got kicked out of a school I hated for drinking before class and I didn't even get in trouble, wow!

Could it really be happening? Were Mom and Dad actually going to start letting me live my own life? But, the fact that Dad wasn't talking to me gave me a very eerie feeling. Had I finally crossed the line? On the one hand, it was a great feeling knowing that I wasn't going to get yelled at anymore, but, on the other hand, I kind of felt unloved. Like they just didn't care anymore. This was a genuine emotional roller coaster. This was not fun! For the first time in a very, very long time, I felt sorrow. I was actually ashamed.

That whole summer I avoided all contact and interaction with my dad. He would get home; I would go downstairs. I didn't get grounded or receive any punishment whatsoever. This made me feel guilty as hell. As the summer ended, my senior year in high school was beginning, and I was really excited to be finishing out my school years back in public school with all my friends. Suddenly, I found myself incredibly bored because all the stuff they were teaching in my classes I had learned two years before at O'Dea. This amazed me, that public school could be so far behind. The thought crossed my mind that maybe I had been getting a good education at O'Dea. Could my father have been right? It was difficult for me to believe that my dad had my best welfare at heart.

Enough of thinking about whether or not I was getting a good education. It was party time! Back with my friends, I was in heaven. It was morning, noon and night smoking weed, drinking booze, and acting up with general disruptive behavior. It was announced at the beginning of the school year that our class of '81 would be the last graduating class of Queen Anne High! All the more reason for the partying with a vengeance.

The entire school year was a blur. Thank God I had gotten a good education at O'Dea, as I didn't have to put forth a whole lot of effort for me to graduate. The entire year was comprised of metal shop, woodshop, technical drawing, and English Literature.

English Lit was my fifth-period class and Mrs. Kilnhofer, my teacher, ended up being the most influential teacher I ever had. She and I had some very deep discussions, and sometimes arguments, about every piece of literature that was put in our hands. I really got into this class because it was interactive between student and teacher, and I took full advantage of this. To this day, Mrs. Kilnhofer remains the highlight of my high school career. She really brought out the creativity, the argumentative and confrontational part of me. Boy, she sure knew how to get my mind working. I loved that class.

The rest of my day was spent screwing around skipping classes more often than not, smoking cigarettes, smoking weed, snorting cocaine and, of course, drinking. I was heading down a very self-destructive and dangerous path that was borderline deadly. I didn't care. I was right where I wanted to be—party, party, party—with no responsibilities whatsoever.

Around late February or early March 1981, while I was constantly in trouble with school and my parents, it suddenly hit me, hypothetically, right between the eyes. Here I was almost eighteen years old, getting ready to graduate from high school and with no clear direction for my life. I wasn't living; I was existing in a fog. I needed to figure out what I was going to do with my life.

I knew darn well as soon as school was out Dad was gonna saw off my corner of the table, hand me a plate and a fork and kick my ass down the road. And, believe me, I deserved exactly that. Fear set in and hit me like a ton of bricks. I had to figure something out, and fast! I stopped smoking weed and snorting coke and cut way back on drinking beer and booze.

I couldn't think of anything that interested me. Then, one day, military recruiters came to the school to talk about how great the military was. All it took to set the hook and reel me in was the phrase "Join the Navy and see the world."

What appealed to me even more was that my grandpa Doug was a retired chief gunners mate in the Navy. All I could think about was that finally, for once in my life, my family would be proud of me! So right after school on my eighteenth birthday I signed on the dotted line. I was excited and anxious to get home to tell Mom and Dad that I had finally done something good in my life. They were both at work, so I set my enlistment papers on the dining room table and then called Grandpa Doug to inform him that I had joined the Navy, following in his footsteps.

When Mom and Dad got home that evening, I got the enlistment papers and handed them to Dad. He read through them with Mom standing next to him and I could see the transformation from disappointment to pride on both of their faces. Dad even told me he was proud of me, and very impressed with my decision. But of everyone in my family, I knew Grandpa Doug would be the most proud of me for my newest endeavor.

I was scheduled to take the ASVAB test (the aptitude test to help the Navy place recruits in jobs that best suited them) in mid-May. I scheduled a physical exam in late June, and my official enlistment date was to be August 12. To me, the most important thing was to refrain from anything that would taint the urinalysis I was sure I would be taking. Between May and June, I abstained from all marijuana use and cocaine use, and only drank beer at parties on weekends.

It took about four and a half hours to complete the ASVAB test, and as I completed it and walked out of the testing facility, I felt really good about how well I did. I headed home elated. I was really looking forward to boot camp. The next couple of months were filled with a whole lot of partying. Everyone who knew me was made aware of the fact that I was going into the military. I got my first taste of being the center of attention among all the kids I knew. Everyone hung out with me and I was invited to every party in the neighborhood.

The impending closure of the high school, coupled with my going away into the service, made for any excuse to party, and I took advantage of all of it. I felt invincible. It felt like I could do no wrong, come home drunk, high or whatever. I had a built-in excuse: "I'm joining the Navy. This is my last hurrah."

Everything I did seemed to be forgiven. To my surprise, my dad sat me down at the end of July and told me that he'd like to have a party for me, and wanted me to invite all of my friends. So Mom, Dad, Trevor and I started preparing this going away party for me. It was scheduled for August 11, and I was leaving for boot camp the morning of August 12. There was a keg of beer, a lot of booze, and Mom, bless her heart, put together a spectacular array of hors d'oeuvres that was second to none. Everything was set up and ready to go and people started arriving around five p.m. The party went on until the wee hours of the morning and there were kids passed out in chairs, on couches, and on the floor. The only thing that really stuck in my mind during that party was how nice it was to be on good terms with Mom and Dad. I was scheduled to be sworn in the next morning at seven-thirty. Well, Mom came running into my bedroom in a panic at nine a.m. "Wake up, Johnny!" she yelled. "You're late for the Navy!"

Dad had a beautiful '67 Camaro convertible, red with a white top, that was to be my ride to the recruiting center. All three of us ran around in a panic to get dressed. There wasn't time for breakfast or anything, and I had a brutal hangover. Dad and I raced to the recruiting center where the enlistment officer had to make special accommodations to swear me in—which he did with a scowl on his face. Once I got sworn in, the waiting began. My flight didn't leave for San Diego until three-thirty. My head was pounding and I actually think I might've still been drunk from the night before, but I was now officially a member of the United States Navy.

The bus picked us up at two o'clock and drove us to SeaTac Airport for the flight to San Diego. Mom, Dad and a couple of their friends met me at the airport to say goodbye and wish me the best of luck in boot camp.

PART
TWO

CHAPTER 6

As I began the next chapter of my life, the US Navy, I was determined to put forth all the effort necessary to succeed in this endeavor, and to make my family proud of the man I was becoming. This was a fresh start for me and I planned to take full advantage of this opportunity. So I walked off that bus at the Naval recruiting station in San Diego, California, "gung ho" and ready to tackle any obstacle that was put in my path.

Feeling the aftereffects of the prior night's festivities, yes, a massive hangover, I was in no mood for any crap from anybody—especially some loudmouth drill sergeant who greeted our bus. He called us a bunch of shitheads and ordered all of us to disembark. I made some comment under my breath as I walked past him. Big Mistake! Definitely not a good way to begin my Navy career. He got right in my face and started screaming, "Who the hell do you think you are?" and told me to drop and give him twenty-five.

I answered, "Twenty-five what?"

Big Mistake Number Two! That was when it really hit the fan, and my hangover didn't help much either.

He screamed at the top of his lungs, "Twenty-five push-ups, you little piece of shit! And they better not be pussy push-ups, because I'll have your ass on that deck until you get them right, if it takes all goddamn night!"

By the grace of God, I remembered how to do a real push-up from gym class in high school. As I was doing my push-ups, all I could think about was how much of an ass this guy was—not even thinking about the fact that I had just walked into boot camp. Boy, oh boy, I was not prepared for this!

When I finished my twenty-five, I decided it was best to just shut my mouth and wait for my hangover to go away. Twenty minutes later we were split up into two companies. I was assigned to Company 185. We were introduced to our company commander, HT1 Horner.

He informed us that for the rest of our lives we would always remember his name. First thing we did was get our uniforms and a seabag. Then we marched to the barracks that was to be my home for the next eight weeks.

The following morning, "Reveille" woke us up at five-thirty. HT1 Horner sat us all down and explained what the next eight weeks were going to entail. The first week was going to be orientation shots, physical examinations, etc. He then announced, "The smoking lamp is lit, smoke 'em if you got 'em."

Everyone who smoked cigarettes ran out to the smoking area and puffed away. HT1 Horner came out and told everybody to gather around him for a meeting. He described the two types of punishment we would receive if we got out of line: The first one was called a short tour, which was three hours of extremely strenuous calisthenics carrying a fifteen-pound rifle and wearing a steel helmet, and a backpack that weighed probably twenty-five pounds. The second and less strenuous of the two was called a marching party, and Horner promised that everyone in our company would go to at least one marching party.

As the eight weeks of boot camp progressed, we learned how to stand at parade rest, attention and at ease. We learned how to march in cadence to the point of becoming a unit. The pride I felt in boot camp, becoming one with everyone in my company, was an amazing feeling. I was actually a part of something good. I watched myself and the other kids in my company transform from a bunch of high school kids with little or no direction or focus, to a fine-tuned machine. It was the most exciting thing I'd ever witnessed.

The night before graduation ceremonies, Petty Officer Horner gathered us all around to tell us he was proud of the fact that we had come so far in the past eight weeks. The sense of pride I felt listening to his words was extremely gratifying. At the end of the speech, he asked the company "Is there anyone here that did not go to a marching party?"

Stupid me raised my hand, extremely proud of the fact that I hadn't been sent to one. Petty Officer Horner saw my hand go up along with one other person, and informed us that we would be going to a marching party that night. I sure felt stupid for raising my hand, especially after him telling us eight weeks earlier that everyone in our company would go to at least one marching party. So, needless to say, I spent the night prior to my graduation from boot camp sweating and marching for two and a half hours.

I woke up the next morning ready to graduate and to become an actual member of the United States Navy. We spent the better part of that day packing, smoking cigarettes, and preparing our dress white uniforms for the coming graduation ceremony. We marched through the ceremony flawlessly, awards were handed out, and everybody's families were filled with pride. My brother and his best friend came to the ceremony to congratulate me for this achievement.

When the ceremony was over, we got our orders and everybody in the company bade each other farewell. We all thanked HT1 Horner for his service and dedication to us. The last thing he said to us prior to departing was that we were not allowed to go to Rosecrans Street (that was where prostitutes frequented) or to the town of Tijuana.

Trevor and Emmett were waiting for me to leave the base so we could go out partying. When I got out, I drank a few beers, we went to dinner, and then headed for Mexico—Tijuana to be exact. It was destiny. Do exactly what I was told *not* to do. Hmm, was there ever a doubt? To my amazement, though, I wasn't too much in the mood for partying and causing trouble. I just wanted to go home.

The following morning I caught the bus to the airport, seabag in hand, heading home for seven days of leave prior to heading east to Millington, Tennessee, for aviation electronics school. I got on the plane headed for Seattle with a whole new attitude about life.

When I arrived in Seattle, Mom, Dad, and quite a few of their friends were standing in the terminal with a banner welcoming me home. I stood tall and proud. This was the most exciting part of my life thus far. All I could think about was *I did it*! I spent that week hanging out with my friends and doing an awful lot of relaxing. Amazingly, I wasn't too much into drinking and definitely wasn't about to smoke any weed. This was the new me, a responsible young adult with a promising future.

The following Monday morning I got on a plane and headed to Millington to begin my training. My life had purpose and I was extremely excited to be learning aviation electronics. Upon arriving at the Naval Air Station in Millington I was given my housing assignment, which was a room with three other students in a dormitory.

Here I experienced hazing for the first time. I set my seabag next to the bunk I was assigned to, and lay down to sleep only to be awakened as I was being tossed out the window—mattress, seabag, and all by the three people who were supposed to be my roommates. I was absolutely livid! I gathered my seabag and mattress and walked back into the room. Not saying a word to anyone, I put my mattress back on the bunk, put my seabag underneath, and lay down again. I wasn't about to start any trouble with anyone, especially after what happened because of my mouth my first day of boot camp.

I went through the daily grind of "Reveille," classes and studying. This schedule stayed the same for approximately four weeks. During this time I found myself getting bored and frustrated with my career decision. I was under the impression when I enrolled for aviation electronics that I would be working on airplanes and helicopters. I was wrong! I was in a classroom soldering circuit cards, nowhere near any type of aircraft.

Instantly, I lost all interest in that school. I tried hanging in there just to finish, but that didn't work out very well either. I stopped doing the projects. No more studying. I ran out of any type of initiative to complete any part of the school. Two weeks later, I opted out. It was a ten-day turnaround to process me out of "A" school and transfer me to the fleet.

As soon as I found out that I had ten free days while I waited for my orders, I borrowed a car from one of my roommates, figuring that while I was in Tennessee I should drive up to Nashville and check it out. So I filled the car up with gas and headed northeast.

Since my dad was a Seattle police officer, he had told me about certain rules, such as what the police can and cannot do when they pull you over. For instance, they can't access your glove box except when asking you for your registration; they can't access your trunk unless they ask to see your spare tire (which was a law in Washington).

So, when I got pulled over by a Tennessee state patrol, he walked up to my roommate's car and in his deep southern drawl said, "Boy, you were speeding" as he reached inside the car. I said, "You can't do that" with a very cocky attitude. He then moved faster than I've ever seen anyone move, snatched me out of the car, threw me up against it, and slapped me, saying "Boy, don't you EVER…."

He startled the crap out of me! I told him that it wasn't my car and gave him full permission to search whatever he wanted to. Incidentally, my cocky attitude disappeared immediately.

CHAPTER 7

The following week I got my orders. I was going to be stationed in Norfolk, Virginia, on the *USS Iwo Jima* LPH2, an amphibious assault ship that was in dry dock in Portsmouth. I caught my flight in Memphis and landed in Norfolk. A van picked me up and brought me to the ship. When we got to Portsmouth I got out of the van and took one look at the ship. *Oh, my God,* I thought, *this massive ugly ship is never gonna float.*

It had huge holes cut into the keel, and the gangplank was a rickety, scary bridge that was about a hundred seventy-five feet up. Walking across that gangplank was the scariest thirty seconds of my young naval career to date. We lived in that dry dock on the boat that would never float for the next six months. It was miserable, but I was stuck there suffering through training, flight deck safety, and mindless cleaning duties.

Finally, after what seemed like an eternity, this tug was ready to float and we were under way for Norfolk.

A week later, we left port on our way to Guantánamo Bay Cuba. Guantánamo was the fleet readiness training/testing facility. We were out to sea for approximately three weeks preparing for our arrival at Guantánamo, practicing everything from general quarters to flight deck operations. At Guantánamo, the training and testing began: eighteen- to twenty-hour days practicing communication skills, flight deck skills, firefighting, and crash and salvage training—in general, battle-readiness training.

We were there for sixty days, and to everyone's amazement we finished this training and testing regiment with a ninety-five percent success rate—not bad for a ship full of misfits. The commanding officer was so happy with our performance that he granted a nine-day liberty stop in Nassau, the Bahamas. This liberty port made me realize that I was right where I wanted to be: in the Navy, going out to sea, then going to a tropical paradise island to party. And boy, did we party!

There was excessive drinking, but the thought of drugs did not enter my mind; that was in my past.

After nine days of partying in Nassau, we headed back to Norfolk. The commanding officer authorized another six-day liberty stop in Charleston, South Carolina. While we were there for six days, there was obviously a lot of partying and brawling between the Airdales and the engineers. Charleston residents were extremely happy to see our ship pull out.

Back in Norfolk, we spent the next ten months in port. Flight deck personnel could not engage in any flight deck operations while the ship was in port, so the Navy would send small groups of us to different schools and land-based air stations for training. Approximately once a month, the ship would leave port and go ten to twelve miles offshore to launch and land helicopters, so the flight deck crew could gain hands-on experience with multiple types of helicopters.

CHAPTER 8

In May 1983, the ship received confirmation that we would be going to the Mediterranean, specifically Beirut, Lebanon. (This experience turned out to change my life forever.) At the end of June, the *Iwo Jima* departed Norfolk naval base headed for Cherry Point, North Carolina, to pick up the Marine amphibious assault unit (MAU). This was a Marine air assault unit, which was comprised of sixteen H46 helicopters, four AH1 cobras, two UH1 Hueys, and four CH 53's (two deltas and two echoes), plus sixteen hundred Marines, thirteen hundred of which were ground forces. Then it was fourteen days of travel to get across the Atlantic Ocean to the Straits of Gibraltar, the entrance to the Mediterranean Sea.

There was a lot of hazing, such as getting sent below decks to get ten feet of chow line from the boatswain's mates, which usually led to getting jumped and tied up and beaten by a few people in the deck department. Once we reached the Straits of Gibraltar, the big joke was to get all the rookies to stand around the flight deck with broom handles to ward off the "sea monkeys."

According to the old-timers, the sea monkeys would stand on rocks approximately a half-mile away from the ship and us rookies had the task of hitting them with the broom handles as they attempted to jump on the ship. Being a new guy I didn't even pay attention to the fact that these monkeys would have to jump not only a half-mile to the ship but up two hundred feet to reach the flight deck. My first thought was, *Where am I, in the land of Oz?* Remember the monkeys with wings? We got through that prank but all of us were the laughing stock among the rest of the ship.

The next five days were spent cruising across the Mediterranean en route to Beirut. The *Iwo Jima* was an LPH2, which stands for landing platform helicopter. So our ship's position was the closest to the shore out of the entire Sixth Fleet. We had the battleship *USS New Jersey* and the carrier *USS Nimitz* in our battle group. Upon arriving off the coast of Beirut, our ship was approximately six hundred yards off the shore and the sixteen hundred Marines disembarked via helicopter. We utilized six landing spots to launch and land helicopters, so it was a nineteen-hour day getting all the Marines off the ship to shore.

There were three jobs in my division, which was V1. We were designated by shirt color. Blue shirts were chock and chain specialists, whose job was to run under the turning helicopter and throw chocks under the wheels and chain the helicopter down. Red shirts were crash and salvage crew. Their responsibility was to fire watch the helicopters as they launched and landed, towing helicopters to the respective spots for takeoff. The red shirts were the guys who wore the silver suit with a gold face shield so if a fire was to start, or a helicopter were to crash, their job was to go into the fire and rescue the pilot and copilot. Then there were the yellow shirts, the landing signalmen who would guide the helicopters with hand signals to properly land them on their respective spots.

I was a blue shirt for the first month of our deployment, which is where everybody starts out. Then they would choose whoever the hardest workers were and promote them accordingly. I worked very hard as a blue shirt and three weeks into the deployment I became the blue shirt lead man. Two weeks later I got my red shirt and became part of crash and salvage. I loved being on the crash crew towing helicopters and parking them, doing maintenance on all of the flight deck equipment, and standing at the ready on the P 16 fire truck during flight quarters. I was overflowing with pride, knowing I was involved in something so important. After two months, I was cross-trained as a landing signalman, basically gaining knowledge of all flight deck operations. This really elevated my sense of pride.

During the next two months, we averaged ten to twelve hours a day of flight quarters duty. My permanent position became crash and salvage. We rotated three three-man crews in two-hour shifts, and during the four hours that we weren't on fire watch, we moved helicopters on the flight deck and assisted wherever needed.

There were eleven Marine casualties ashore during this time frame, five of which were friendly fire. After flight quarters we would sit up on the back catwalk and watch tracer bullets (bullets with red phosphorus coating, every fifth one in a clip) fly through the air and occasionally one would hit the water by the ship or on rare occasions actually hit the ship, not causing any damage because they were 7.62mm rounds.

With six Marines being killed or wounded by the Shiite Muslims, I don't need to tell you that tensions were escalating between us and the radical Shiite Muslims. Things became dangerous from enemy fire so we were all ordered to wear flak jackets while on the flight deck. Throughout the month of September, we remained at flight quarters an average of fourteen hours a day with deck temperatures over 100 degrees. Wearing those heavy flak jackets and the silver firefighting suits was extremely demanding physically. Now I know what it feels like to be a frozen dinner being heated in a microwave oven.

The cobra gunships were in the air constantly serving as protection for the aircraft that were taxiing Marines back and forth from sea to shore. The Shiites upped the ante mid-September by bringing in fifty Cal machine guns right on the shoreline and taking shots at helicopters flying overhead. The cobras stayed very busy every minute we were at flight quarters, providing cover fire for the 46s.

One day in late September, one of the cobra pilots, whose call sign was Bulldog, was providing cover fire for a 46 and two Hueys when Bulldog called the ship to let us know he had taken two rounds, one in the oil cooler and one that had nicked the tail rotor shaft. Bulldog was so pissed off that he turned his gunship around and fired two Sidewinder missiles at the trailer responsible for hitting him, blowing it to smithereens. But his gunship was badly damaged and losing oil quickly so he hurriedly came back to the ship.

He came down the flight deck so hard that the skids folded out and the helicopter was sitting on the Gatling gun. The blue shirts ran in and chained the copter down tight. Within seconds the tail rotor shaft snapped, jerked the helicopter sideways, and knocked Bulldog out when his head hit the canopy. To make matters worse, a magnesium fire started and the crash crew was forced into action. I drove the P 16 to within twenty feet of the helicopter and sprayed it with firefighting foam while the two guys in my crew pulled Bulldog and his copilot to safety.

The only way to put a magnesium fire out is to jettison it, pushing it off the ship! We got the crash crane to release the chains and pushed a forty-seven million dollar helicopter off the side of the ship. Bulldog regained consciousness and began hooting and hollering about how we got those bastards that shot him.

The following day, our ship was ordered to go one mile off the coast because the *USS New Jersey* was going to threaten the area with a show of power, firing their sixteen-inch cannons into a hillside. That evening, we pulled anchor to get out of the line of fire, but our ship went dead in the water so they had to cancel the *Jersey's* "fireworks" show.

The following week, *Marine One*, the vice presidential helicopter, brought Vice President Bush and the Secretary of State on board to assess our situation. They spent the day in meetings. The ship's crew was briefed the following day by our respective department heads. The general consensus was that because we came into this conflict as a "multinational peacekeeping force," we were not given the authority to lock and load or fire on the enemy until fired upon. This upset an awful lot of our ship's crew because Marines were getting killed and wounded by the Shiite Muslims without our having the ability to defend ourselves. Very frustrating! Six more Marines were killed within the next ten days.

Usually, when a ship goes on a cruise they generally hit a liberty port every thirty to forty-five days, but because we were in this conflict there were no liberty ports. Instead, the ship authorized a barge and flew all of us onto that barge on a Saturday afternoon and gave each of us two beers, letting us hang out, relax, and drink our beers. There was a small group, a skeleton crew that stayed on the ship during this time to maintain readiness. The fighting continued to escalate for the next eight days, yet we were never given the authority to lock and load our weapons, essentially rendering us unarmed. We were like sitting ducks. With the Marines constantly being in harm's way and the long hours we were putting in—coupled with the lack of sleep all of us were suffering from—most of the crew was on edge and easily agitated. There were a lot of arguments and some fighting among shipmates.

Saturday, October 22, 1983, the entire ship's crew was informed that Sunday was going to be a day of R&R. The ship was anchored and there would be no flight quarters all day. When flight quarters ended Saturday afternoon/evening, I headed to the squadron's aviation electronics locker to see my buddy Dave, a Marine who was one of my closest friends on board the ship. Dave and I had become friends at the beginning of our deployment, mainly because he played the guitar, and was very good at it. I played bass guitar, if that's what you want to call it. I wasn't very good, not for lack of trying because I practiced and practiced, but I didn't have any musical talent at all.

Dave and I met every evening and played guitar together, and he tried his best to teach me how to play better. That evening, I got to his work area and found out that his wife in North Carolina had had a baby girl the week before. He had a letter from her with a picture of the new baby. Dave was on Cloud Nine. That was one proud father. I congratulated him and asked him what his plans were for the day off. He said he had gate duty at the BLT (Marine barracks on shore) from four to ten a.m. So we made plans to hook up on the flight deck after his duty was over. I congratulated him on being a new father and told him I'd see him the next day after his watch. That was the last time I ever saw Dave alive. I went to my berthing area and sat down and watched some TV for about an hour then went to bed.

At six a.m. Sunday morning, I woke up to the blare of the air horn and the announcement over the ship's loudspeaker: "General quarters, general quarters." (General quarters is announced only when the ship is under attack or in imminent danger.) It was immediately followed by, "This is not a drill, this is not a drill. All hands, man your battle stations. This is not a drill. This is not a drill. General quarters, general quarters, all hands, man your battle stations."

In a panic, everybody got out of their bunks, quickly got dressed, and went to their respective areas. My assigned area was obviously the flight deck. Flight quarters was announced. Unaware of what the situation was, we all worked diligently preparing the flight deck, getting CH 46 helicopters on every spot and ready for takeoff. I had no idea what was going on but I realized that the training that we had down in Guantánamo Bay was about to pay off. All our drilling, training, and practicing made the entire crew's movements to reach their battle stations effortless.

We launched all six helicopters and prepared six more for takeoff. Then it was announced over the ship's intercom what the emergency was—a truck full of plastic explosives had crashed the gate and rammed the BLT, exploded, and caused the entire barracks to implode!

There was no time to think; just to act and react. Ten minutes after launching the second set of helicopters, the first set returned and as each one landed teams of two people would go out and unload the dead and wounded off of each copter. As soon as the bodies were off-loaded, the helicopter would take off again to retrieve more bodies.

Our ship had been designated the medical receiving facility for the carnage that had taken place onshore. As they brought the bodies on board, they were covered with silver blankets but the rotor wash would often blow the blankets off as we were carrying them to the elevators in order to lower them to the hangar bay, which had become a giant operating room.

As I was carrying one stretcher off a 46, the blanket blew off the body and all I could see was one eye that appeared to be staring at me. The remainder of the head was half gone. For a split-second I gazed into that eye and deep inside my heart knew that the body I was carrying was my friend Dave. But there was no time to think, just act.

This went on all day and night for more than three days. Copter after copter, body after body, they just kept coming. We lived on that flight deck nonstop flight quarters for the entire time. They brought us sandwiches and coffee from the mess hall every couple of hours, and in the late afternoon and early evening we were sent down for a short time to get supper, the one hot meal for the day.

Going down to that chow hall required going through the hangar bay, which had become a giant operating room with wall-to-wall stretchers and bodies. Doctors and nurses frantically worked, trying to salvage what little life was left in most of these guys. We dug deep into our souls and went on, no matter how exhausted we had become. Amazingly, everybody went on working well over seventy-two hours.

Even to this day, I have no idea how that whole crew continued working during that time almost mechanically. The only emotion I felt was sheer pride; there was no time for sorrow or mourning for our comrades. Everything that day was automatic as every takeoff and landing was executed flawlessly, no matter how tired we were. Today, remembering the events that took place now thirty years ago, it still raises the hair on the back of my neck, gives me butterflies, and quite often brings tears to my eyes. There was a sense of pride that not many people experience in their entire lives, let alone at the age of twenty.

Soon after the initial massive influx of dead and wounded were brought aboard, we were sent in groups of eight ashore to dig through the rubble searching for the remains that were still missing in action. As our helicopter landed at what was left of the BLT, we disembarked with our shovels to do the unthinkable: retrieve body parts, look for dog tags so we could identify them. Obviously everyone searching would be looking for any signs of life.

On October 27, the orders were given that everybody on shore was able to lock and load while on duty or on patrol. An investigation took place over the next two weeks as to what happened the morning of the bombing. Evidently, a yellow Mercedes pickup truck with 35,000 pounds of plastic explosive in the bed circled the barracks multiple times before circling wide one last time and turning sharply towards the sentry on duty—Dave—accelerated, and crashed the gates. The truck's passenger took out both gate guards with an AK-47 as the truck crashed through the gates at a high rate of speed, hit the stairs going into the entryway of the BLT, and exploded, causing the center of the building to collapse and the two outer sections to implode into the gap that was created by the collapse.

The most upsetting part of this whole ordeal to me was the fact that both Dave and the other guard saw the truck circling the building and radioed it in to the duty sergeant, voicing serious concern about what that truck was up to. When they realized what was happening as the truck headed straight for the gates and accelerated, it was too late. The clips for their side arms were buttoned into one side of the duty belt and the pistol was buttoned into the other side, making it impossible to load, aim and fire on the approaching vehicle.

Two hundred and fifty-two Marines were killed that day. Thirty years later I still firmly believe that this carnage could have been avoided if Dave and his partner had only had permission to load the clips in their pistols. I pray every day for those casualties. May you all rest in eternal peace.

Everyone I worked with on the flight deck was absolutely floored not only by what we had just been through, but knowing that this whole thing could've been avoided. That just pissed everybody off even more. After that week, you could see a definite shift in attitude among everybody on the flight deck. There were no more smiles, no laughing in the chow line, no joking around, or a goodhearted hazing for anybody. The mood throughout the ship for the remainder of that cruise was extremely somber.

The *Iwo Jima* was relieved by the *USS Inchon* in mid-November. The Marines from HMM 12 were all brought aboard the ship and we headed home. The twenty days it took to get through the Mediterranean, the Straits of Gibraltar, and across the Atlantic, seemed like twenty months. Everybody on board, Marines and sailors, all felt defeated and exhausted.

Although this was a horrible tragedy and as a twenty-one-year-old man with a deep depression that seemed overwhelming at times, I had this strong, unwavering love for the United States of America, and the mission that was dropped in our laps was for the greater good of the world.

CHAPTER 9

As we pulled into port at Cherry Point, North Carolina, we were greeted by multiple high school bands waving banners and flags welcoming us home. They were marching, singing and cheering. The Marines and all their equipment disembarked and the ship pulled out of port and headed for Norfolk, Virginia. This was the end of the most mind-numbing, deeply depressing period of my life. Restful sleep was difficult to come by because I kept replaying the six a.m. call to general quarters and the four days that followed in my mind over and over again throughout the course of every night.

Once we returned to Norfolk, we were granted an excessive amount of liberty due to the trauma we had experienced in Lebanon. All of my close friends and I began partying, heavy drinking morning, noon, and night. We would go to morning muster, work for three to four hours cleaning spaces and maintaining flight deck equipment. Then it was straight to the bar and drink until the bars closed. But no matter how much alcohol I consumed, I couldn't get the pictures of all the dead and wounded Marines out of my head.

I also purchased a motorcycle soon after returning from Beirut. A lot of the guys that knew me on the ship were convinced I would be dead in no time because of the reckless behavior I exhibited. My life revolved around drinking, riding that bike as fast as I possibly could, popping wheelies, racing wherever I could to get an adrenaline rush! And, of course, chasing women every night while I was barhopping. I did everything I could to erase all the horrible things that my eyes had witnessed overseas.

One night, after a heavy night of drinking, as I was riding my motorcycle down Ocean View Boulevard on my way back to the base, I got pulled over. After doing the field sobriety test I was arrested and given a DUI ticket. The following morning, after spending the night in jail, I went in front of the local magistrate. I'll never forget this experience because his name was Judge Lawless. He had a deep southern accent and when I went up in front of him he looked at me and said, "Boy, where did you get your license, Jack Daniels University?"

I was released on personal recognizance and got the ticket reduced to negligent driving. Over time, my license was suspended for reckless driving, drinking and driving, and once I even got into a high-speed chase running from the police.

One day, as I was leaving a local watering hole called The Drifters, my friend Val and I were walking up to his apartment after a day of drinking and as we were walking up Ocean View Avenue, I spotted a '73 Mustang Grande convertible for sale on the side of the road. They only wanted five hundred bucks for it so Val and I stopped and looked at it. It was the middle of July and hot as hell. The top was down. All I could see was a money-making opportunity: Fix it up. Sell it for approximately ten grand. So I bought it. No haggling or trying to talk them down; I just bought it. I signed the papers and Val and I got in, fired it up, and drove up to his apartment.

When we got there we both got out at the same time, and with both doors open the car sagged almost to the ground. The frame was completely rusted out. I hit the power top button and to my surprise when the top came up it was nothing but a frame. So Val and I went to the store and bought a carpet needle twine and a big piece of Naugahyde and three hours later my Mustang had a top.

The following Friday night, we decided we were going to have a toga party. We took four full-size garbage cans and loaded them with chopped fresh fruit, grain alcohol 190 proof, and any other booze we could find. We poured the booze in the garbage cans over the chopped-up fruits and let it sit for a day and a half. We were totally smashed by five p.m. Seven of us, wearing togas, climbed into my convertible and drove up the main drag, hollering toga, inviting everybody we saw on the road. How we didn't get arrested and go to jail that night is way beyond me.

Val and I shared the same duty night on board the ship. We lived together, worked together, and had duty together. We worked a regular day and realized that the reason we were so bored was because we were stuck on the ship all night. This was part of duty; you had to spend the full twenty-four hours on board the ship. One night, he and I were down in the berthing area, watching boxing or something, I think, and we had the bright idea that we would shadow box each other. So we were playing around shadowboxing when Val stepped forward, took a swing, and accidentally hit me in the mouth. He broke my front tooth and cut the back of his hand wide open. We wrapped it up and went to see the on-duty corpsman. He sent Val down to the hospital to get stitches and a few hours later he came back with his hand all wrapped up, stitched, and he had a bottle full of really good painkillers.

Two days later, his hand was so swollen that I took him to the hospital and they told him he had to go up to Bethesda Naval Hospital in Maryland to get the wound reopened because it was infected. I felt responsible so I decided that I would give him a ride up in the Mustang. We grabbed a case of beer and hit the road north for the four-hour drive. It was a beautiful day and we had the top down. About two hours into the trip, on painkillers and beer, Val had the bright idea that while we were doing sixty-five, he would climb over the windshield and lay on the hood. Not a good idea, especially with only one decent hand. Once again we were very lucky that we didn't get hurt, killed, or pulled over and arrested. That car got impounded six months later when the police pulled me over because it was unsafe for the road.

CHAPTER 10

In August 1985, I was riding my motorcycle down a main drag, not paying attention and speeding. The road ended and turned into a gravel parking lot with a chain-link fence at the end. I stood on the brakes at about forty-five miles an hour and the bike slid across gravel and then flipped, throwing me off and pinning me against the chain-link fence. The foot peg went into my leg, right next to my shin. I got major road rash on my forearms and elbows, not to mention my knees and the palms of my hands. I was taken to Portsmouth Naval Hospital, where they put me on pain killers and cleaned the road rash with scrub brushes and iodine. They sewed up my leg and wrapped it in gauze, then admitted me to the hospital.

Completely whacked out on morphine, nothing mattered to me anymore. With not a care in the world, I lay in the hospital bed and hit the morphine button over and over again. The second morning I was in the hospital, I had just eaten breakfast when my groin started hurting. Within thirty minutes, my groin had swollen to the size of a softball. I hit the panic button and screamed for the nurse. She came in, took one look at the groin, and started prepping me for immediate surgery. Evidently, when they sewed my leg up there was rubber residue from the foot peg still in the wound and the infection was traveling up my leg in a hurry. My lymph node had swollen because the infection was traveling so quickly. They opened my leg back up in surgery and cleaned everything out of it. They left it open for ten days, doing fresh saline flushes every two hours and stuffing saline-soaked gauze into the wound. They loaded me up with intravenous antibiotics.

After stitching me up, they observed me for twenty-four hours and then released me with a big bottle of pain pills and orders not to ride a motorcycle. So of course the first thing I did was buy another motorcycle. I ended up at a bar that night on my new motorcycle, pain pills in hand, and began drinking heavily. Mixing the pain pills with the alcohol got me stumbling drunk quickly. My new motorcycle ended up sitting in the parking lot that night because there was no way I could even hold the bike up, let alone try to ride it.

The next morning, I got up, popped a couple of pain pills, and headed for the bar with the full intention of picking up my motorcycle and going back to bed for the day; actually following doctor's orders by keeping my leg elevated. I got to the bar to pick up the motorcycle and noticed a couple of my friends' cars, so I don't even need to explain what happened next.

Yes, I ended up sitting on a bar stool for the rest of the day, drinking. Four days later, I went to the doctor's office for my follow-up appointment. He looked at the wound in my leg and the road rash, and left the room. Twenty minutes later, I got the diagnosis: I was going to be on shore duty for the remainder of my Navy days.

I wanted no part of that. If I couldn't go to sea, I wanted out of the Navy, but I didn't say anything. When I had healed enough to go back to work, I was assigned to a shore-based squadron at Ocean View Naval Air Station. I spent the entire next year drinking, partying, and shirking responsibility. I did not see eye-to-eye with my chief petty officer in charge, so that made matters worse and I was falling back into my rebellious, nonconforming attitude again.

Even though I was rebellious and not happy about my situation, I thought I could fight back and figure out a way to get back to sea and return to an aircraft carrier. The chief put me on projects such as cleaning bathrooms, buffing floors, and picking weeds. This was not my job and I hated going to work every day.

My friend Val had been transferred to shore duty also and he was stationed in Ocean View at the same air station. But Val wasn't attached to a squadron; he was attached to supply. A couple months after my assignment to HM 12, I came to work hung over from partying the night before, and I was ten minutes late. The chief wrote me up and I went to Captain's Mast (non-judicial punishment), given fifteen days restriction, half my pay for one month, and fifteen hours extra duty.

During that fifteen days restriction, we had our dress white inspection. I was on my way to this inspection (I had to walk because I was not allowed to drive my car or ride my motorcycle while on restriction) and I got a couple of spots of dirt on the lower leg of my dress uniform. So I was late and I failed the inspection. It was back to Captain's Mast again. I was awarded another fifteen days restriction, half my pay for a month, and because I hadn't completed the fifteen days extra duty from the prior's mast, they didn't give me any extra duty. I did my best to complete all of my punishment. I made it through, somehow!

Two weeks after getting off restriction, I came to work one day and during morning muster, the chief informed our squadron that the base commander was going to be doing a walk-through the following week so we had to work on getting all of the passageways in the hangar shipshape. Knowing that I had a good friend in the supply department, right after muster he called me into his office and asked me if I could get some good wax and a good buffer and pad. So I called Val and he said yeah, he could get it, but he was leaving at noon to go partying. I told the chief what was going on and the chief told me if I could get the buffer, the wheel and the wax, I could have the rest of the day off too. Absolutely, I was all over it!

I called Val and told him I needed all the equipment right away and then I would go partying with him at noon. I delivered everything to the chief and informed him I was leaving.

"Have a good night," he said. "And, thanks for expediting everything."

Val and I partied the rest of the afternoon and most of the night. I went to work the next day and to my surprise I had yet another write-up from the chief. The bastard wrote me up for "unauthorized absence" for the half day he gave me off. Unbelievable!

Well this time I wasn't going to Captain's Mast. They were sending me to court-martial. I headed straight for Judge Advocate General (JAG) to get an attorney. I met with the attorney. I was less than thirty days from my EAOS (end of active obligation of service). The attorney informed me that in his opinion there was no way they could process me out before my release date. Bad Advice. They had me processed out in nine days.

Three more motorcycle accidents, relatively minor ones; multiple speeding/reckless driving tickets; two Captain's Masts later, I wore out my welcome in the United States Navy. They processed me for court-martial to kick me out of the Navy in Other than Honorable Discharge for administrative reasons. This was January 1986.

PART
THREE

CHAPTER 11

O nce they escorted me to the gate, I got on my bike and headed over to my friend's house and asked if I could sleep on his couch for a couple of weeks. By drinking to excess, I depleted my savings account and all the cash I had on hand. After all my money was gone, I got a job working at a construction site in Virginia Beach. Within a week of working there, I made a couple of new friends. We drank together and partied together. Two weeks later, I was reintroduced to the world of cocaine. After two months, I lost my job, was out of money again, and had no place to go.

My dad told me about an underground cable installation company in Richmond, Virginia, so I telephoned the owner. "If you can get to Richmond, I'll hire you," he said.

I had one last night of major partying to do: lots of cocaine, lots of booze, surrounded by people I didn't really care for. We partied for three days, bade each other farewell, and I loaded my seabag, strapped it to my bike, and headed for Richmond.

Two-and-a-half hours later, I arrived in Richmond, stopped at a gas station, and called my soon-to-be new boss, Tim. He told me to wait there and arrived twenty minutes later. I followed him to his house and to my amazement he had a room set up for me to stay in until I could find a place of my own.

The following day was my first day on the job. I was now a ditch digger, something my mom warned me of while I was in school: "If you don't study hard and get good grades, you're going to end up being a ditch digger." Funny how things work out, huh?

The job was very labor-intensive and physically demanding. I spent the better part of the first week swinging a pickax. What was funny about this company was that it was based in Colbert/Savannah, Georgia, and half the crew had a Bob at the end of their name. It was Billy Bob, Jim Bob, Joe Bob, and Phil was the crew boss, so jokingly I called him Phil Bob, a name that stuck.

After the first day of work, everybody went back to Tim's house and drank a lot of beer and ate barbecue pork rinds with Tabasco sauce, which created the need for even more beer. Everybody and their crew worked incredibly hard and played just as hard. Within two weeks I moved in with Rodney and Troy. Everybody called us the three amigos. Tim's brother Sonny was the lead man of our crew, with the pecking order being Phil as the boss, Sonny next, and Rodney, Troy and I the crew.

Over the course of the next two years, we dug a lot of underground cable from Richmond, north to Washington, D.C. We even did one job up in New Haven, Connecticut, which was a lot of fun because it was College Town USA with Harvard and Yale right in the area. Needless to say, we did an awful lot of drinking, which led to a lot of problems with the law, disorderly conduct, drunk in public, etc. etc.

One day I was riding my motorcycle from the job site to our house, trying to get home to change into some decent clothes because we were going out to dinner that night with Tim and his wife. As I rode down the freeway at about seventy miles an hour, I noticed a minivan up ahead that was swerving badly; my first assumption was that the driver was drunk. He was taking up all four lanes, going side to side. I waited until he reached the far right side and I went to the far left, downshifted, accelerated, and popped the clutch. Suddenly, the front wheel came off the ground and I kind of panicked, let off the throttle, and in a split-second the driver was back over to my side of the freeway! My left hand and handlebar hit his right rear tail light, the bike flipped and threw me. It felt like I was in suspended animation as I slid down the freeway. It seemed to take forever as I kept thinking I had slowed down enough sliding and ripping all the skin off my arms and legs that I could go into a roll and minimize the road rash. This happened like four times before I finally was going slow enough to roll to a stop.

The asshole in the minivan stumbled out of the driver's seat and staggered up to me. "Are you okay?" he slurred.

I had a dislocated shoulder and an awful lot of road rash. I wanted to kill him. I chased him but I was having some difficulty running as my legs and arms were so chewed up. Just then a constable pulled up in a Virginia state patrol car. I was out-of-control, screaming at this guy. The police officer placed me under arrest, took forty dollars out of my wallet and gave it to the gentleman to replace his broken tail light, and arrested me for driving under the influence—leaving my totaled bike in the median of the freeway.

They took me to the station to administer a breathalyzer and of course I blew a 0.00, then released me from the holding cell, still bleeding with a dislocated shoulder and an awful lot of pain. They told me I was free to go. Extremely pissed off, I called Tim and asked him to come get me and take me to the hospital, which he did immediately.

While I was getting cleaned up and bandaged I showed Tim the police report, and he informed me that the guy I hit was a board member with the state police or some such thing, which pissed me off even more. I went back to Tim's house, signed my title over to them, and asked him to buy me a one-way ticket to Seattle in exchange for my motorcycle. I packed my stuff and headed for the airport. Once I got to the airport I contacted my mom and dad and let them know I was moving back home to Seattle.

When I arrived, my parents and a friend, Rita, were there to pick me up. At baggage claim I spotted my mom and walked towards her. She looked past me. I said, "Mom, it's me, Johnny." I guess the full beard, mustache, headband, and long hair made me pretty unrecognizable. As we drove home across the viaduct, there before us was the most beautiful sight I had ever seen—Seattle Center, the Space Needle, and the downtown Seattle skyline. It was great to be home.

Within a week of my arrival, I got a job working for an insulation company in Fremont, a small neighborhood near Lake Union. I worked there for approximately six months, hanging insulation and getting paid by the foot. Nasty work, low wages.

Then in January 1988, I got a job working for a nationwide restaurant supply and food distribution warehouse in Kent, in the freezer department picking orders. There were a select few guys that I really got along with. I got an apartment in Auburn, another suburb between Tacoma and Kent. Within a month of living there, I was doing cocaine almost every weekend and partying way more than I ever had before. The only difference was that this time around I wasn't partying for partying's sake. I was attempting to hide the depression and emptiness that the ordeal in Beirut had left with me.

The scars on my heart were deep and painful and the only solution I knew was to drink and drug to oblivion. If I wasn't able to remember my own name, I thought I could erase the past. The more I drank and snorted, the easier it became to cope with reality, which had become a blur. Pretty soon, the Friday and Saturday night forays turned into Friday, Saturday, Sunday and then almost a daily ritual—indugling all night and most of the day, working from five p.m. until six a.m. and then starting again. About every three days I would sleep for twelve hours.

It wasn't long before I met a girl named Nell and instantly fell for her, but it was two weeks prior to a ski vacation I had planned with three of my coworkers. We had enough cocaine and booze to get us through that seven-day trip to Salt Lake City. We skied at different resorts and were high the whole time and drunk most of the time. All I could think about was Nell and I couldn't wait to get back to see her. When we got back she picked us up at the airport.

She and I began a relationship and this was my first real relationship with a woman. We moved in together, rented a house in Maple Valley, and all I could think of was "and they lived happily ever after." She was a real trooper, drank with the best of us and did cocaine with all of us. To my surprise, Nell was the first person who successfully changed my focus off of Beirut. Her family and mine went on a four-day golf vacation together to Lake Chelan. I discovered I was really falling in love with her; my parents and everybody in my family really liked her. We even went to South Dakota on a hunting trip and Nell and I got along fabulously. Still, everything in my life revolved around cocaine. Nell and I stayed together for close to two years, during which time she cleaned houses and I worked graveyard at the food services company. We had a lot of parties at the house in Maple Valley.

On a Saturday afternoon, Jerry, a coworker, came over to my house and asked if I wanted a line. "Of course," I said, and grabbed the mirror we used for snorting. He put out a little line and chopped it up. I grabbed the straw and snorted it up my nose. Now, just to let you know, when you start cocaine it instantly numbs your nostrils, but this time when I started the line it burned the inside of my nostrils as if I had just sniffed fire up my nose. I panicked.

"What the hell was that shit? It burned like hell, dude!"

Jerry very calmly looked at me. "It's crank."

I was angry for a second but as soon as it took effect I was like

"Wow"; my heart raced more than it ever had while doing cocaine. I liked this crank a lot, and thirty minutes later my heart was still racing and, unlike cocaine, I wasn't thinking about another line. I really liked this stuff! I had heard of crank but had never given it a thought because I was pretty fond of cocaine.

Nell came home a couple of hours later and Jerry and I were high as hell, in the middle of shooting a game of pool. She walked down to the basement and said Hi. I told her I had a surprise for her. She was excited, thinking that I was going to throw a line of cocaine out on the mirror that she spotted on the table. (She knew we were high because that mirror was not put away.)

Jerry gave her a line, but before she snorted it I told her it was crank. Her eyes lit up. "I *love* crank!"

Evidently she had been doing it off and on for quite some time. No wonder the house was always so clean when I got off work at six in the morning. Sometimes she would be vacuuming or wiping down the kitchen at six or six-thirty after I'd come home from working all night. She did a couple of lines so now all three of us were high. Hours later, I was still higher than I'd ever been. I loved this shit!

I went outside and washed and waxed my truck, mowed the lawn, and cleaned out my garage. This crank was amazing, I loved it. The whole rest of the day and night I didn't sleep, and all day Sunday I still wasn't tired. I lay down, knowing I had to go to work at six o'clock that evening. I was getting frustrated because I knew I needed to get some rest, but sleep was not anywhere in my near future.

Oh, my God, two days wide awake with no hope or desire to sleep. When it came time to go to work, I headed in and put in the whole night working, still wide awake. After work, I headed home and crashed hard, out like a light. I woke up fourteen hours later, two hours late for work, and ended up calling in saying I was sick.

For the next six months, I learned how to smoke crank off of foil with a straw, and how to make glass pipes so I could smoke the shards. I spent all my time either high on crank, getting high, or looking forward to the next time I was gonna get high. Over the course of the next couple of months I went from doing crank on the weekends to a couple of times a week to being a daily user. It seemed like Nell and I were getting high all the time. For some strange reason, I was able to keep my job, barely, occasionally using sick leave and vacation, but still employed.

One night after work, I got home, went through the front door, and saw a bullet hole in the ceiling right by the front door. I asked Nell about it.

"The feds were here knocking on the door and I got the gun to keep them out. It went off as I was walking to the front door," she said.

Nell had become ultra paranoid from using meth/crank, always thinking that somebody was outside the house trying to get her—the feds, police, dealers, whoever. I installed a home alarm for her to feel safer and we got a dog. After six months of this paranoid lifestyle, I couldn't take it anymore so I decided to leave her. I packed my stuff, just what I could fit in my truck, and moved out.

I had purchased a boat, a 1972 Jolly Roger cutlass, while Nell and I were together. It was a sixteen-foot speedboat that was very fast. Two friends of mine, Theo and Carl, were heading to Eastern Washington to watch the Hydro races in Tri-Cities and asked me to join them. I decided I needed a vacation and agreed to go with them. To this day I don't know why, but we all three took our own boats—three guys, three trucks, three boats.

After we went over the pass and arrived in Yakima, we stopped for a bite to eat and decided that we would leave my boat at a yard owned by the company I worked for. Theo's boat was a tournament ski boat, and Carl's was a cabin cruiser, so there was no need for my boat. We got to the Columbia River in the Tri-Cities, grabbed a bunch of beer, and launched Theo's boat. It was nine o'clock in the morning, and the party began. We sat out on the water and drank well over two cases of beer, then proceeded to go water skiing. The water was kind of rough and we were all pretty hammered but that didn't stop us. This went on for about two hours with not much luck getting any good skiing in. So we loaded the boat up on the trailer and headed to a Mexican restaurant for dinner and shots of tequila.

About nine-thirty that night, absolutely out of it, we all three decided that we needed to go skiing. So we headed for the boat launch and dropped the boat into the water. This time we had a fifth of booze each, and the boat had lights, so what more did we need?

By the time we got the boat on the water it was probably ten-thirty or eleven. We took turns skiing. Theo went first, I drove, and Carl spotted. Theo had no luck getting out of the water, so he came back on board.

Then it was my turn. I jumped in the water, put my ski on, grabbed the rope and yelled "Hit it!" I had no luck either getting out of the water for more than maybe a minute before falling down. So I got back on the boat and it was Carl's turn.

Now just to let you know, Carl was a little guy, weighing only about a hundred and thirty pounds, so we couldn't feel the boat waver when he made the cut. Theo was driving and I was spotting. Carl yelled, "Hit it," and off we went. We could both hear Carl hooting and hollering but we couldn't see him; it was too dark. Theo drove the boat at close to full throttle for what seemed like about ten minutes. Theo asked me how Carl was doing.

"I have no idea. I guess he's doing okay."

About five minutes later, I grabbed the rope and gave it a tug, Carl wasn't there! Theo immediately backed the throttle off and turned the boat around as I pulled the rope in. Where was Carl? It was so dark out on the water we couldn't see a thing. We had no spotlight. All we had was the bow and stern lights, so we zigzagged back and forth up the river trying to find Carl.

It took about thirty minutes before we found him. He was just floating in the water, drinking out of his fifth that he had tucked into his ski vest. "Geez, it took you guys long enough," he said.

He thought it was really funny while Theo and I were pretty freaked out. We thought we had lost our little buddy. We decided it might be best to bring the boat out of the water. It took well over two hours for three drunken idiots to get the boat on the trailer, and it was a miracle we didn't get arrested.

The next day we watched the races. Sunday evening, after all the festivities were over, Theo and Carl loaded everything up and prepared to head back to Seattle because they had to work Monday morning. I was on vacation for a week, so I rode to Yakima with Theo, and when we got there I got in my own truck, said goodbye, and headed for Lake

Chelan. I spent that week barhopping and boating by myself or with anybody I made friends with along the way. It ended up being a really great vacation. I had money, drugs, a boat, and a week with nowhere to go and no one to answer to!

A week later I was back at work. I stayed with my friends Drake and Bonnie, so that really curbed my ability to get high all the time. My drug use tapered off, but my drinking began to get out of control again. Drake had a jet ski that we played around on a lot, since I had gotten rid of my boat a couple of months earlier.

Another coworker of mine, Thad, had a tournament boat, so we spent a lot of time going out waterskiing. Lake Washington, Lake Tapps and Lake Meridian were our favorites. One Thursday evening after work, Drake, Thad and I decided to go skiing on Lake Meridian, so right after work we took the boat there and launched it. Naturally there was a lot of drinking going on because it took quite some time for boat traffic to subside so we could get some smooth water to ski. Finally, about eight at night the water had calmed down enough.

I threw my vest on and started putting my gloves on when I realized that my diamond ring was still on my finger. This was a three-quarter carat diamond solitaire that was investment quality. I had traded it for some drugs a couple of months earlier. It was worth about five grand. I never wore any jewelry while skiing for fear that the rope could snag a ring and rip my finger off, so I took the ring off and handed it to Drake, about to ask him to put it in the glove box. Before I could get the words out, Drake, who was so drunk he didn't realize what I had handed him and thinking it was a bottle cap, threw it over the side of the boat.

The following day we hired a diver with a metal detector, which was a futile effort because there was four to five feet of silt at the bottom of the lake. The diver informed us that there was no way in hell we would ever find that ring.

My friend Drake also had a house in Bingen, Washington, near the Oregon border. We would go down there and do work around the house, do some golfing and, naturally, an awful lot of drinking. We would go down approximately one weekend every two months. There was a Chinese restaurant/bar across the Columbia River in Hood River, Oregon, that Drake and I frequented when we were in Bingen. The restaurant had a specialty drink called the scorpion. It was extremely strong and came in a big trough with long straws. It was designed to be consumed by four people, and there was a two-scorpion limit.

Drake, myself and two friends we had gotten to know headed to Hood River via a little fourteen-foot speedboat that one of our new friends had. We headed right for the Chinese restaurant to drink a scorpion or two. Five scorpions later, we decided to head back across the river. Doug was so drunk he opted to walk across the bridge rather than get in the boat to cross the Columbia. This proved to be a very smart move on his part, because we were all pretty stinkin' drunk. The three of us jumped in the boat, fired up the outboard, and headed across the Columbia. That's the last thing I remember until I woke up the next morning in the boat that was stuck on a sand bar. My two friends were passed out too. We had evidently forgotten to turn the auxiliary fuel tank on, and the boat died in the middle of the river.

Wow, we could've ended up lost at sea, but for some reason the boat drifted near the shore and wedged itself on a sand bar. We hooked up the auxiliary tank, pushed the boat off the sand bar, and motored up to the boat launch. Somehow Drake made it to the house, a miracle in itself. I'm guessing that all four of us were pretty lucky that night that we didn't wind up dead or lost at sea.

CHAPTER 12

Summer ended and fall arrived. Grandpa asked me if I wanted to go elk hunting with him for a week. I took a week's vacation and we headed up to Highway 410/Crystal Mountain. Drake and Bonnie did not smoke and neither did Grandpa. I was trying to quit so I thought it best to do it while I was up in the woods with my grandfather.

Three days into the hunting trip, however, I decided I wanted to smoke again. I headed down to Enumclaw for cigarettes, stopped in a Chinese restaurant/bar to have a drink and smoke a cigarette.

That's where I met Cathy. She and I danced, drank, and hung out for the rest the night or at least until the bar closed. We then got invited to an after-hours party. I never even gave Grandpa a second thought, and whether or not he was worried about my not showing back up. All I knew was that there was meth/crank at this party so the next three days were spent with Cathy snorting/smoking meth and partying.

Three days later, I called my mom and my grandpa to let them know I was okay. Everybody was just plain angry since they didn't know whether I was dead or alive. I don't think Grandpa ever forgot that week. I did a terrible thing to my whole family but it didn't matter because I was right back in the crank game.

Cathy and I began dating and I stayed with her in her trailer in Black Diamond most of the time. Four months into our relationship, Cathy told me she was pregnant. I was excited to be a father. She quit using during the pregnancy, but I continued to use crank but kept my use hidden from her. Seven months into the pregnancy, she informed me that I probably was not the father because she had been sleeping with her ex-boyfriend. I was shattered. I moved out and stayed with my friends Randy and Jerry. The cocaine, crank and drinking got to mammoth proportions once again.

In the meantime, I had been hired by an airplane manufacturing company as an electrical installer and was promoted to functional test technician after being hired. I did not get along with my supervisors because I was still using during my time there.

One day, I was working on some landing gear testing and I found a couple of problems at work related to overheat detectors and reported them to the immediate supervisor of that area. He became angry when I basically told him that his people weren't doing their jobs correctly. He told me it was not my concern to worry about anything that wasn't directly related to the job I was doing in the landing gear area.

"Flight safety issues are *everybody's* responsibility!" I replied.

We got into a little bit of a heated discussion about what my responsibilities were. Now, this altercation happened two weeks after a plane had crashed off the coast of Southern California and eighty-one people were killed so with that being fresh in my mind, I said, "Why don't we call the families of the eighty-one dead people that fell out of the sky two weeks ago and ask *them* if it's my responsibility to worry about flight safety issues."

I was terminated 45 minutes later for insubordination.

Josh was born on October 30, 1996. I had to prove he was my child by DNA testing and it came back 99.9 percent positive that he was my child. I decided to forgive Cathy for her infidelity. As time went on, it was difficult because I realized that you could forgive all day long but you never forget when somebody has cheated on you.

We both got right back into meth as soon as Josh was born. We used every weekend. When Josh turned one, we decided to get married, so we left him with my parents and went to Reno. Eight months later, Cathy was pregnant again. We bought a house in Edgewood because the trailer was no longer big enough for a family of four.

At that point, I began shopping for a minivan, yes, a minivan. I found one down at a car lot in Puyallup, a small town very close to Edgewood. It was a '96 Nissan Quest in very good shape, so I ran home, picked up Cathy and we went back together to look at the Nissan. She liked it too so we told the dealer that we would go home and think about it and let him know the next day whether or not we wanted to buy it. Cathy went to work the next morning, called me on her lunch break, and told me to go buy the van.

When I got to the dealer I noticed in the back of the parking lot an '89 Mustang Saleen convertible. I wanted that, car, badly!

So I negotiated with the dealer and bought both of them. I made the mistake of driving the Mustang home instead of the van. When Cathy saw it, she became unglued. I tried explaining that I got a really good deal on it, but it didn't matter—she was furious.

A few months later, on June 10, 1999, Charlie was born. Cathy again had stayed clean during the pregnancy while I maintained my meth intake secretly. Cathy chose to breast-feed Charlie, but we found out later that her milk never came in, so there were no nutrients going into Charlie's body.

The Fourth of July weekend we went to my mom and dad's condo for a fireworks party and my dad took one look at Charlie and told both of us we'd better get him to the hospital ASAP. He had lost over a pound and a half. He was only six pounds, six ounces when he was born, so a pound and a half was a lot. We took him to Children's Hospital the next day and they admitted him immediately. I spent the entire week at his side, drug-free.

The hospital was doing approximately one test per day trying to figure out what was wrong with him. I got angry at the staff because I didn't think they were doing enough for my son. I was kicked out of the hospital and immediately went down to the condo to talk to my dad. He told me they were doing all they could and Charlie was in the very best possible hands he could be and the only thing I should do was go up there and tell him I loved him and be by his side. He had lost so much weight and was suffering from so much malnutrition that they didn't give him much of a chance. I sat next to him and kept repeating how much I loved him and urged him to hang in there. Miraculously, he started eating rice formula slowly, then a little more every day, and before too long he was up to seven pounds and getting released from the hospital. Cathy and I decided that we would cut way back on the meth use, but I still did as much as I had been all along, only in secret.

For the next two years the kids would go away to either my parents' or Cathy's parents' house for a weekend at a time and she and I would get high. One Sunday, after we had been doing drugs and playing cards all night long the night before, when it was time to go get the kids we stopped using. About an hour later, Cathy came down to the garage and asked me for another line. I told her no because she had to go get the kids. We got into a huge argument but I stood my ground. No more drugs! She became angrier than I had ever seen her.

She left to go get the kids about four p.m. I was putting a new engine in my Camaro so when she got back about an hour-and-a-half later I rolled out from underneath my car to say hi and that I would be up in a few minutes. Five minutes later, she walked out of the garage with the kids and got into her car.

"Where are you going?" I asked.

She said, "I'm going to get dinner."

"Okay, bring me back a burger and I'll be ready to play a game or something when you get back."

That was the last I saw of her for over two weeks. I got divorce papers the following Tuesday afternoon. Once again I was shattered and my life spun out of control. I spiraled downhill so fast that I was using all day every day. Soon I had a bunch of less-than-honorable people living in my house.

I bought a Honda CBR 900 from a meth addict not really caring whether it was stolen or not. I just wanted to go fast. I was riding across the I-90 floating bridge and two bikes pulled up alongside me, revved their engines, downshifted and took off. The race was on! I downshifted two gears, revved the engine and popped the clutch. The front wheels immediately came off the ground, and as soon as I was fully inverted and I ran out of gas, the front end came down so hard the fairing broke. I coasted approximately two miles to the gas station, cheating death once again.

There were always cars coming and going at my house because some of the guys that lived there were dealers/meth cooks. With all the traffic in and out of the house, I knew that sooner or later the house was going to be raided. That day came in November 2001. When I answered a knock at the door, I was greeted by at least ten policemen. As they came in, I asked if they had a search warrant and one of them pistol-whipped me. I fell to the ground and they stormed the house, tearing everything apart.

One of the guys living there had a couple of meth manufacturing implements, hoses, propane tanks, and muriatic acid. That was enough to arrest me and they took me to jail. I spent the next two-and-a-half months trying to beat the case but it wasn't going to happen. Meth was the hot topic throughout Washington at that time.

Finally, in the first week of February 2002 I was released into the "breaking the cycle" program, random UAs and tests plus meetings. I lasted about three weeks before using again. Every time I had to pee in the bottle, I drank bleach first to clean out my urinary tract. That worked for a while but then I got caught, and had to do the remainder of my year in county jail.

I got released in August 2002 and moved in with my brother. A longtime friend of his, Sammy, was building a hair salon and he hired me to hang a couple sheets of drywall. I pretty much worked day and night helping Sammy and his wife construct this salon. I stayed clean for approximately six months; went to work for an appliance installation company, delivering and installing major home appliances. I liked the job and it kept my mind off of doing drugs. But every single morning I was one phone call, one step away from going back to drugs. Every day was a battle of wills; I think this is what they call "white knuckling" it.

Basically, all I was doing was existing, looking for an excuse to use meth. In February 2003, I got the excuse I was looking for. I had just purchased a 2001 Dodge Intrepid and was heading from Bellevue, east of Lake Washington to Mountlake Terrace, a town north of Seattle. My partner, Alex, was driving the delivery truck and I was driving my Intrepid going across the 520 floating bridge. There was traffic merging up ahead so I had my left turn signal on and noticed a state patrol car behind me switch to the left lane to allow the traffic to merge. The state patrol was about a hundred yards behind me. I got past the merge, flipped my turn signal on again and changed lanes to get back in the right lane. Suddenly, he hit his lights and pulled me over. I pulled over to the park-and-ride and shut off the engine. The officer then came to my driver's side window and asked me to step out of the car. He said he believed I was inebriated so I did a field sobriety test, passing all phases of it with the exception of following his pencil with my eyes only. The sun was right behind him and I guess I was squinting when I did it; therefore he arrested me for driving under the influence of marijuana.

I didn't smoke marijuana and I had been clean for six months, so I got argumentative with him; this was a mistake. Two more police cars arrived, one with a drug-sniffing dog. They tore my Intrepid apart while one officer grabbed my laptop off the passenger seat, slammed it on the roof of the car, and asked me for my password. By this time I was extremely angry because the dog was scratching the hell out of my car while sniffing for drug evidence. The officer typed in my password, looked at the computer for a few minutes, then angrily slammed the lid down, cracking the case, and threw the laptop on the passenger seat. The dog found nothing but had scratched the black paint terribly with his claws. I was then handcuffed and put in the back of the police car. They left my car unlocked, the windows down, my laptop on the passenger seat, and the keys in the ignition. They left my car at the park-and-ride and arrested me for driving under the influence of marijuana.

I was taken to the Roanoke substation. A drug recognition expert met us there, put me inside a dark room, and instructed me to stand still, keep my eyes open, and then he hit me with about a million candlepower spotlights. The drug recognition expert pointed to the arresting officer saying that my eyes had radically changed.

I was furious. "That's what they're supposed to do with severe change in lighting."

The arresting officer said that he wanted me to submit to a blood test. I agreed and told them to take me to the hospital. He replied that he was going to be the one drawing the blood and I said, "No, I will not allow a state trooper to stick a needle in my arm."

"So, you're refusing?"

At that point I asked if I could call my father.

"Is your dad an attorney?" he asked.

"No, he is a retired Seattle police officer and I want to ask him if this is standard operating procedure."

Then he replied, "You cannot make a phone call because this is a drug-related arrest. The only person you can call is an attorney."

So I refused a blood test, he punched my license, and said I was free to go. I had no idea where I was so I asked if I could have a ride back to my car and was told that if I was caught going near my car I would go to jail. An officer said he would give me a ride to a familiar place. He dropped me off at a Jack-in-the-Box at 85th and Aurora in North Seattle—the drug-dealing, prostitute capital of Seattle! I called my dad from a payphone and he sent my brother to pick me up. Trevor took me to my car and I followed him home.

The next morning I went to a clinic to have a urinalysis and a blood test. The results came back 0.00. I went to court three weeks later, taking the lab results with me. Yet I was still found guilty because the judge said that with my criminal record she was not going to side against the police officer.

So they found me guilty of DUI, I thought, *even though I white knuckled for the past six months. The hell with it.* And off to the dope man I went. I hooked up with several other users and resumed the drug life.

We were cooking very large quantities and selling it for a huge profit. I got hooked up with Samoans and Ukrainians, which were the most ruthless drug addicts and dealers I had ever met. On multiple occasions, I had guns pulled on me and I pulled guns on others. It was a dog-eat-dog nasty world I was involved in. I was right back at it, cooking and selling it to support my habit, which had gotten pretty serious.

For the next seven months, I was making a lot of money buying whatever I wanted and doing a lot of dope. I was basically homeless, going from meth house to meth house, getting a shower once a week or so, and trading fake IDs for money to fund my meth cooking ingredients. I was on a self-destruct path, down to a hundred and forty-five pounds, also known as being sucked up. My life was spiraling out of control and I believe I was on a death march. I did not care in the least as long as I could stay high. The running and gunning and reckless behavior I was engaged in went on for six months. I dealt with people who were disgusting, dirty, and foul.

During that time, I began dating a girl named Dixie. She was very cute and I almost immediately fell in love with her. She prided herself on being a car thief and a computer whiz, and she was a self-proclaimed master of forgery. She and I became inseparable. I loved this girl with all my heart. I bought her a Toyota Celica GT, which was stolen two weeks later. I was driving a Datsun 300ZX and she rode with me everywhere.

One day she and I went over to another drug addict's house because he evidently had some software on how to make fake IDs. Without thinking, I let my guard down and pulled into his driveway with no means of escape in case something went wrong. We went into his house to look at the software. While there, knowing that I had five hundred dollars in cash on me to buy the software, he pulled a gun on me and Dixie. I told him the money was in the car so we walked outside; I told Dixie just to walk casually to the passenger side, get in and put the keys in the ignition. As I walked to the driver's side, another car pulled up behind us and blocked the driveway. I quickly got in and started the car, put it in Reverse and hit the gas. I slammed into the car behind me and pushed it across the street through a garage, put the Datsun into first gear, and hauled ass out of there. The whole back end of my car was dragging the ground because it was totally smashed. We drove it approximately five miles then parked it and left it; now we were on foot. We ran through yards and fields for about two miles, and when Dixie couldn't run any farther I picked her up and carried her rather than leave her behind. We reached a friend's house in Auburn and spent the night there.

The next day, while she was still sleeping, I went to get my Mustang. I returned before she woke up and loaded what we had left from the day before into the Mustang's trunk. When she woke up we headed to my friend Andrea's house and asked if we could stay there for the night because we were on the run. This was okay with her as long as I gave her some dope.

About two o'clock in the morning, we heard the bullhorns. The police had arrived in the neighborhood, surrounding Andrea's house. Dixie and I hid underneath the bed, perfectly still for well over five hours. They never found us but they arrested Andrea's boyfriend. When we finally did get up and get out of there Dixie looked at me and said she had never felt more safe than when she was in my arms. A week later, she took off with another guy! Needless to say, once again I had a death wish. I didn't care about anything or anybody. Slipping into a deep depression, I started to feel like I was really dying.

So for the next month I smoked more and more and more dope trying to kill myself. This gut-wrenching, mind-numbing pain just seemed never to want to leave. I couldn't shake it no matter how hard I tried. I went away with two friends and cooked up a large, large batch. Four days later, I was back in town with well over twenty pounds of methamphetamine.

I was in my friend's house dividing up my mess into smaller baggies when one of my Ukrainian friends came over and asked me for some dope. I asked him how much he wanted and he said about a quarter-ounce, so I scooped out what looked to be close to a quarter-ounce and gave it to him.

"How much do I owe you?" he asked.

"Don't worry about it," I replied.

He took it, walked out, and five minutes later I felt the cold steel of a 9 mm touch the side of my head and heard the hammer go back! He told me I had shorted him. I told him to kiss my ass because I gave him the drug for free. I also shouted at him, "You'd better never pull a gun unless you intend to use it!" He was stunned by my total lack of concern. I didn't care about anything. As far as I was concerned, my life was over anyway at that point.

Sometime around late August or early September 2003, I went on a five-day bender, ending with crashing for close to two days. I woke up lethargic, exhausted and hungry. I looked at my meth pipe, my little baggie and dope, and got sick to my stomach, I could not do this anymore. I needed a change quickly. So I threw my pipe and my baggie in the garbage and stomped on it, went back inside the house I was staying at, lay down and slept for another two days.

After four days of doing nothing but sleep, I woke up and started my new life...or so I thought. I didn't change any of my friends or the people I hung out with; I just wasn't smoking the dope anymore. I continued selling meth and living the same lifestyle, and hanging out with the hard-core dealers and addicts. This seemed to work out fine for the most part, but it didn't take long before I realized how foul the meth game is. These people would steal anything that wasn't bolted down. Pathetic! I realized how truly disgusting this life was.

The paranoia that addicts displayed was almost laughable. Every car with tinted windows was a fed, and God forbid if the news helicopter flew overhead. It had to be the police undercover. Over the course of the next four months, I ran around town selling dope, constantly asking myself the question, "Why the hell am I doing this?" But I was now accustomed to that lifestyle.

Another three months went by quickly, and I was going nowhere. My life was at a standstill. The divorce was final and I was spending very little time with my kids, because there was always one of the addicts or dealers with me. I had rented a small apartment with another dealer and we were making a lot of money selling drugs.

CHAPTER 13

O ne day one of my Ukrainian friends came by our apartment to hang out and to get some dope. He and I went to the local Honda dealer and he waited in the car while I went in to buy a helmet. Victor was driving. It had been raining the night before so the roads were a little bit slick, so as we left the car lot, he hit the gas a little bit hard and spun the tires. A Federal Way police officer saw this and pulled us over. He ran a check on Victor's license and discovered it was suspended. I told the officer that I had a driver's license, and I would be willing to drive his car home to save him the impound fees. So the police officer asked for my driver's license, which I gave him immediately. He walked back to the police car and within minutes there were four other police cars there. He walked to the passenger side with his gun drawn and ordered me to step out of the vehicle.

"We've been looking for you," he said, and placed me under arrest. Unbeknownst to me, there was a warrant out for my arrest.

When I went to court the following Monday morning, I found that there were warrants out for me ranging from forgery, to identity theft, to manufacturing and delivery of a controlled substance, namely methamphetamines, forty-two counts in all. As I fought the case over the next two months, I thought for sure I was going to beat it. For one, Washington State criminal court rule 3.3, speedy trial rights, stated that out of custody when they file an indictment they have ninety days to bring you in front of a judge. They filed my indictment one hundred seventy-four days prior to bringing me in front of a judge.

Second, everything that they were charging me with was based on hearsay: addicts getting pulled over with tiny amounts of meth telling on me to stay out of jail.

And third, there was no evidence except a blurry photograph of some guy with glasses and full facial hair cashing a stolen check.

In my opinion, this wasn't nearly enough to convict me. I was threatened with one hundred eighty-nine months in prison. The prosecuting attorney came to me with an offer of thirty-three to forty-three months, a drug offender sentencing alternative, basically cutting my time in half. So essentially I was looking at eighteen months and I'd be out. So I talked to my attorney and agreed to take the deal. The judge came in about twenty minutes later and asked the prosecuting attorney if she had struck a deal with me. She replied that she had and handed him the plea agreement I had just signed. He asked me if I understood everything that was written in the plea agreement. I told him that I did.

Before proceeding with sentencing, the judge looked at me and said, "I don't usually grant drug offender sentencing alternative (DOSA) sentences to anyone that hasn't gone through treatment or at least put some effort toward becoming drug-free. Therefore I am not going to grant you the DOSA, and I am not about to cut your time in half without seeing something that shows me that you're serious about quitting drugs."

I objected immediately and my attorney looked at me like I was crazy and told me to be quiet. I was not allowed to object; only she was. I explained to her that I was very aware of the U.S. Constitution, and I had the right to freedom of speech which I was invoking right then.

The judge asked me where I objected. "Your Honor," I began, "you are an idiot, because if you would have taken the time to read through my file prior to becoming God, judge, and jury in deciding what my fate was going to be for the next couple years, you would see that I have been through treatment at sundown M Ranch in Yakima."

The judge scanned my file and he was visibly upset and angry because I had just called him an idiot. He replied, "I see you have been in treatment. Sundown is a very good facility but I am still not granting you a DOSA sentence. I'm giving you forty-three months, the maximum I can give you under the sentencing guidelines. You will do forty-three months in a correctional facility. If I could guarantee that you will do every minute of that forty-three months I would, but the State has mandated that you will get some time off for good behavior. Get him out of my courtroom!"

I'm thinking that calling the judge an idiot probably wasn't the smartest thing in the world I've ever done, but it seemed like the thing to do at the time. BIG MISTAKE! Three days later, corrections officers shackled and chained me up for transfer along with fourteen other people who were making the transition from county jail to state prison. We were shuffled onto the bus and headed for Shelton, the receiving facility for all of the Washington state prisons.

When we arrived there we were sent directly to classification based on our crimes. There were three receiving units numbered one through three, and three more numbered obviously four through six. The first units, R 1-3, were the primary units and 4-6 were transitional housing. The receiving units were way overcrowded. Every two-man cell had an extra inmate in it. I was put in R1, which was designated for LWOP (life without parole); 23-hour lockdown with one hour out each day for yard, and a shower every other day. It was miserable. I tried to make the best of it, making friends with my cellies in the two adjoining cells.

I was very new to this so I wasn't aware of some of the prison etiquette, or the code. Three of my newfound friends and I were walking around the track in the gym during our one-hour yard, but I was walking the opposite way and a guy bumped me as he passed. He called me a punk bitch. I just kept on walking not even thinking twice about it. The guys I was walking with informed me that I had to do something about that because punk and bitch are the two most unacceptable words someone can use in the prison environment. I was told that if you let somebody call you a punk or a bitch and you do nothing about it you will become one.

Being the new guy, nervous, and not too sure about what I had gotten myself into, I listened to them, turned around and followed the guy into the bathroom, grabbed him by the back of his head, and slammed it against the sink. His forehead split wide open and blood went everywhere. I casually turned around and walked out of the bathroom. Thirty seconds later, corrections officers came out in force and told everybody to lie on the floor face down as they sent the medics in to tend to my victim. They strip-searched each and every one of us and sent us back to our cells on lockdown, pending an investigation. I never got caught for that altercation, but I did notice an immediate change in the way people looked at me and treated me. I think I gained some respect that day. We were on lockdown for seventy-two hours then it went back to the usual routine. That was the only real problem I had while I was in R1.

Three weeks later I was transferred to R4. This was between six and eight hours a day out in the yard, going to a chow hall for meals rather than having the meals brought to our cells, and with my drug-dealing history and relatively high profile I had maintained in the drug world, there were an awful lot of people there that I knew. Some friends, a few enemies, and even a couple of people that told on me, a.k.a. snitches. In all my time in the drug world I never pulled any underhanded crap, or ripped anybody off. In fact, I had a pretty good name in the drug world. This made my time in prison relatively trouble-free.

On a couple of occasions I ran into people who told on me; they all knew I knew what they had done so it seemed like they avoided me like the plague. I was even asked occasionally by the people I spent time with on the outside what I would do if I ran into any of those people who had snitched on me. My reply was always the same: I wouldn't do anything or I would thank them for saving my life, because I knew if I didn't make the changes in my life and disassociate myself from anybody that used drugs that I was sure to fall right back into the game again.

After five weeks of the R units, I finally got my transfer documents to Cedar Creek Corrections Center. The following Thursday I was shackled and chained to four other inmates this time, loaded on the chain bus for transfer to Cedar Creek. Cedar Creek was a work camp, for wild land firefighting and forest maintenance. Upon arriving at Cedar Creek, I noticed there were nowhere near as much security, razor wire and guard towers at this facility. It was a minimum-security camp. When I got arrested four months earlier I was one hundred seventy pounds; by the time I went through county jail and the receiving units in Shelton, I had ballooned up to two hundred fifty pounds, so I was not in very good shape.

The first thing we did when we got out of the chain bus was to head for classification and sign up for the jobs we wanted, I signed up for DNR (Department of Natural Resources), the fire crews. Then we got our housing assignments and proceeded to our respective bunks in the dormitory. In order to get on the fire crew there was a physical agility requirement called the "pack test." It was more of a stamina test than an agility test; you had to wear a thirty-five pound backpack and walk briskly, without running, forty laps around the track, which was a total of approximately three-and-a-half miles. I completed the pack test with a couple of minutes to spare. My upper legs felt like spaghetti and my shins felt like somebody had just beaten them with a baseball bat. Everybody who completed the tests that day, including myself, was exhausted but proud.

I was assigned to fire crew 63. On the first day I went to the supply room to get all the gear needed for forest maintenance. This included work boots, a hard hat, safety glasses, and extra clothes. The first day was basically safety training on operating a chainsaw. The crew was made up of the crew boss, who was an employee with the Washington State Department of Natural Resources, not a corrections officer; a first lead; a second lead; and eight workers.

The first day on the job everybody in the crew mocked me because I was so big and overweight. We hiked up the side of the hill with our chainsaws, cutting all the lower foliage, thus giving all the trees room to grow. If there were groups of trees too close together, we would cut down the smaller ones. This was a very tiring job, physically demanding, and I was exhausted at the end of the day. But little did I know the crew had a surprise for me. All nine of them jumped me and tied me up, but I put up one hell of a fight. Eventually they did get me tied up and proceeded to give me a pretty good ass-whipping. It was kind of like hazing in the Navy or a rite-of-passage. Once again I proved myself because I fought back, and even though they won and got me tied up, I didn't go easily. In fact, my fighting back caused a few bloody noses and assorted cuts and abrasions. And once again I was a part of something. This seemed to be a pretty easy way to do a prison sentence.

Wild land fire season started usually around late May or early June, so the month prior we did what they called controlled burns and dug trails. My prior firefighting experience from the Navy didn't really do me a whole a lot of good for forest fires, but I had found myself really enjoying this work, not to mention the fact that I had trimmed down to two hundred pounds and I was actually in very good shape. Whenever there was a fire east of the mountains or anywhere else at a distance, the crews would go for twenty-one days at a time and fight these fires.

In July 2003 there was a big fire in Tanasket, Washington, and our crew along with four other crews dug trail for eighteen days to contain the fire. We then headed back to the prison and were back for three weeks doing forest maintenance when a huge fire erupted at Lake

Chelan and crews from all three state correctional facilities arrived to fight it. It took four weeks to contain that fire but the crews only stayed for three weeks because, as I mentioned, twenty-one days was the maximum. We fought local fires just about weekly, mostly from lit cigarettes that people threw from car windows. When we weren't putting out fires, we continued to thin the forest. We spent some time on standby to see if the local fire departments needed any help.

In late October and early November the next phase of our job occurred: tree planting. Each inmate on our crew was responsible for planting three hundred and fifty trees a day, which was not an easy task at times. Some guys on our crew were slower so others of us picked up the slack. Each crew was supposed to average thirty-five hundred trees a day. Rain, sleet, snow, ice, it didn't matter; we planted trees every day.

On December 1, 2003, the Washington state penitentiary system decided that smoking cigarettes was no longer allowed in any state facility. I was in a panic because I did not want to quit smoking so I started making phone calls to try to find somebody to help me get tobacco inside. A friend lived near where we worked every day, so I set up a deal with her to drop tobacco off and made sure that whoever I sold it to would have their friends on the outside send money to her. So I set up the drop spot and lined up sales to other inmates who wanted to continue smoking. She would buy the tobacco for a dollar forty a pouch and I would sell it for twenty dollars a pouch. Anybody who wanted to buy from me would have twenty bucks sent to her and as soon as I got word from her that the money was there I would give them their tobacco. This turned out to be a pretty lucrative deal for her and I always had tobacco, a win-win situation.

As time went on, the corrections officers all caught on to the fact that I was selling the tobacco and they tried their damnedest to catch me, but it never happened because I always had other people hold for me. The deal that I had going kept me smoking and my locker was always full of candy, hygiene articles, and anything I wanted. Once again I was the big man on campus, so to speak. Everybody knew who I was and that if they needed cigarettes I was the go-to guy. This arrangement had its own set of problems, however, because guys who got caught smoking cigarettes would immediately tell the corrections officers that they had gotten the tobacco from me.

I couldn't believe it! My God, it seemed like there was no "honor amongst thieves" anymore. I've watched a lot of movies and TV episodes where the story had a criminal element, and guys never squealed on each other! If you got busted, you did your time; you didn't tell on others. Your friends took care of all your personal stuff and made sure that you always had what you needed while you were behind bars. Boy, in my experience, that was the farthest thing from the truth.

During my entire time in prison, I wrote letters to my kids and ex-wife almost weekly, and repeatedly asked Cathy to bring the kids down to visit me as my mom and my grandfather came to visit quite often. Mom could verify that it was not a bad environment for the kids. Finally, after two-and-a-half years she agreed to come down with my mom to check it out for herself. Afterwards, she acknowledged that it was not what she thought at all and promised to bring the kids to visit me. But, I waited for the remainder of my sentence for her to follow through with this promise. She never came.

In early August 2006, donations were collected from the community surrounding the prison, which facilitated the purchase of backpacks, pencils, pens and assorted school supplies for the children of the inmates. The prison put on a carnival for all the children so I sent the flyer to Cathy and told her it was going to be fun and there would be games for the kids. I begged her to bring the boys. She filled out the necessary paperwork in June so I spent the next two months eagerly awaiting and anticipating a reunion with my children.

On the day of the carnival, all the inmates who had family coming to this event were shuttled up to the baseball field. We all sat on the bleachers awaiting the arrival of our families. At nine a.m., families started arriving and as each busload off-loaded the kids and their mothers the inmates joined their families. Ten o'clock. Eleven o'clock. Soon it was noon and the festivities were full in swing. Still I waited. I sat on that bench watching all these families enjoying their kids. I was the only one left sitting on the bleachers. .No Cathy, Josh or Charlie.

This was quite possibly the most depressing day in my prison sentence. What made it even worse was that I was stuck there to watch all of this because there was no transportation back to the prison. I couldn't believe that Cathy would promise to bring the kids and, knowing how excited I was, just not show up. At that moment in my life, I firmly believe that if I had had access to a gun, I probably would've ended my life. It felt like everything that was positive in my life had been sucked out in that one afternoon. I lost all my drive. I had no will to go on; nothing mattered. Compounded with the tragedy in Beirut, the situations I had gotten myself into in the drug world, and the prison sentence, everything was becoming too much to handle. For the next two weeks, I didn't have any desire to keep pushing forward. This was the most crushing blow I had ever felt.

The rest of my time in Cedar Creek was spent dodging the corrections officers and avoiding getting caught being the tobacco cartel. They searched my cell almost daily. Every day I came home from work I would find my cell had been torn apart; yet they never found anything. I had the bulk of the tobacco stashed in the washing machine control panel, and my personal stash was kept under the edge of the base molding all the way around my cell. I had rigged dental floss down the post of my bunk where I would keep the rolled cigarettes and my lighter.

All the corrections officers were very aware that I was smoking pretty much at will and they had a pretty good idea that I was the one responsible for the influx of tobacco at the facility. A few weeks before I was to go on work release, I was in the bathroom taking a leak when two corrections officers stormed in and had me grab the wall while standing for a search. They stripped me down and proceeded to pat me down. I felt that one of the officers kept his hand in my private region a little longer than necessary, borderline fondling. I played this one up to the fullest.

I went to my counselor and put on an act that would've gotten me an Academy Award. I walked into his office shaking and told him I had been violated; that I felt dirty. He told me that if I filed sexual harassment charges of any kind against any of the officers, they would take my work release away and I would serve out the remainder of my time in Cedar Creek. He assured me that it would be a miserable existence for that last six months of my sentence. So needless to say, there would be no charges filed by me. I got my transfer documents and headed for Bishop Lewis work release in downtown Seattle on September 20, 2006.

This was another big change in my life, a fresh start. I went through the orientation, got the rules and regulations and prepared myself to go job hunting the next day. I woke up early the next morning and hit the bricks. I walked all through downtown Seattle putting in job applications. This went on for well over a week. At the end of the first week my counselor had me in her office explaining to me that with my construction abilities and qualifications, I should be able to find a job soon.

The following week I finally got a job offer from the Ramada Inn in downtown Seattle as a maintenance person. I went to work immediately. Believe it or not, I enjoyed the job immensely. The only drawback was I worked with a bunch of Armenians, which took me back to the Ukrainians I dealt with in the drug world. This could have been a trigger to draw me right back into that game which had already cost me nearly five years of my life. I worked a lot and soon was promoted to chief maintenance engineer at the hotel. My evenings were spent playing cards and watching TV. As long as I kept my mind occupied, the depression from all of the stuff that I'd seen and been through in my life stayed in the back of my mind. I found myself sleeping very little and multiple times every night waking up from nightmares and bad dreams about guns being pulled on me and people dying all around me.

After my first week at my job, I was allowed to apply for eight-hour furloughs. These were sponsored temporary releases from the work-release facility. My mom was my sponsor and she would come down and check me out for the day, giving addresses and full itineraries of the activities that I would be doing during the time away from work. Josh and Charlie were both playing Little League football and Cathy had given us their game schedule.

My mother and I chose a Saturday to come down to the football game. I had high hopes of starting to rebuild the relationship between father and sons. Mom picked me up to go to Maple Valley to watch my kids play football. As we pulled into the parking lot of the football field, Cathy met us in the parking lot and began screaming and hollering at both of us, saying that we weren't invited and to get the hell out of there. She called my mom quite a few foul names and yelled that my kids didn't want to see me. This was in front of approximately fifty parents and twenty kids on their way to their respective games. This was extremely embarrassing to both my mom and me.

I calmly walked up to her and reminded her that she had invited us and had told us of the schedule for this particular game. She screamed quite a few more expletives toward both my mother and me.

We decided it was best that we leave because the last thing I needed was any kind of trouble on my first furlough out of prison.

This was a crushing blow dealt by my ex-wife. Josh's birthday was a week and a half away and knowing that I wasn't going to see him on his birthday I had purchased some gifts for him and Charlie. I had mentally prepared for a heartfelt loving reunion with my children only to have it destroyed by their mother.

I wasn't sure I could take much more of this heartbreak in my life. I felt like the bad choices that I made in my past had completely ruined me and the thought of going on trying to do the right thing was just not going to happen. I went back to the work-release totally shattered and depressed. What else could go wrong in my life?

For reasons I can't explain, I found the strength somewhere within myself to forge ahead. The Ramada was doing a full remodel/renovation and I was given a lot of responsibility to oversee this project. For the remainder of my time in work-release I spent every day working at the Ramada and every evening planning the next day's work.

During that six months I was building a decent little savings account in the work-release bank.

My scheduled release date was February 14, 2007. Valentine's Day! I found that rather amusing getting out of prison on Valentine's Day! I began making phone calls to rent an apartment. I was determined to do this on my own without the assistance of my parents.

The task of finding a place to live with a felony on my record proved to be quite a challenge. For two weeks I made over two hundred phone calls and the answer was the same from every one of them. Once they asked if I had any felonies or criminal convictions or if there was anything they would find on my background check and I was honest and said yes, their reply was always "No, we don't rent to felons."

I did find a couple of places that didn't have management companies running them so there was a chance, but they wanted to meet me first and do an interview. On February 13, I woke up with the flu. My God, what else could go wrong!! I stayed in bed and took the day off from the Ramada. The renovation was nearly complete anyway. The morning of my release I was still feeling pretty crappy. I packed all my personal belongings and went for my pre-release interview with my counselor, an hour and a half of questions and answers.

The last question she asked me was, "Is there anything you can think of that will make you reoffend?" My response was, "If anybody goes near my kids, I'll kill them."

This was yet another major mistake in my life. My counselor instantly changed my status to "dangerous and violent felon." She informed me that if I had any violent behavior in the next five years I would go right back to prison—no questions asked. This was not a good way to start my new-found freedom.

I gathered all my release papers and picked up my check from the savings that I had accrued while working at the Ramada. I almost collapsed when I saw the check. I had saved $4100 during that six months. I opened up the envelope and in it was twenty-five dollars. I asked where the rest of it was and was told that it went to child support, back child support, that is! I then learned that I had accrued $41,000 in back child support during my time in prison. Life just kept getting better; yet another crushing blow at the hands of my ex-wife.

The thought of getting a place to live with twenty-five dollars was definitely not going to happen. Mom came and we loaded all my personal belongings in the back of her truck and departed the prison system, hopefully never to return. We drove down to the Ramada and I humbly begged my boss to give me a room for a while, asking them to take it out of my paycheck. My boss was very sympathetic to my situation so she agreed to let me stay in a room as long as I needed to free of charge. What she did to help me out with that room was the spark I needed to stay focused on remaining free and not falling into the revolving door of the prison system.

It's amazing how much a small bit of generosity from my boss meant to my succeeding in the beginning stages of my freedom. I packed what little bit of stuff I had into the elevator and headed to room 512, my new home, at least for now. Mom and I went to lunch and then the real work began. She took me to the Department of Licensing to get all the forms needed to get my driver's license back, went to DSHS and applied for a new social security card. I used my mom and dad's address as my permanent address of record. I didn't have probation or parole so there was no need to report to a corrections officer or check in with the probation department. I was finally done with my sentence. Or so I thought.

PART
FOUR

CHAPTER 14

On the morning of February 15, 2007, I woke up in my motel room, took in the Seattle skyline, and had a warm feeling about my new-found freedom. I actually could come and go as I pleased. After a shower and a cup of coffee, I headed downstairs to go to work. I worked every day, even on weekends, so I could earn enough money to buy a vehicle and find a place to live. I stayed in the hotel for a little over a week and finally found a couple that was willing to rent to me. They had a small mother-in-law house right behind their home, which made it very easy for them to keep an eye on me if necessary. My mom went with me and we both left a very good impression. The rent was five hundred dollars a month. They didn't require first and last month's rent, just a five-hundred dollar damage deposit, so I scheduled my move for March 1 and gave them the first month's rent. We made an agreement to have the damage deposit paid in full by the time I moved in.

Now the next challenge I faced was finding a vehicle to get me back and forth to work. Phil, one of my friends from school owned an auto repair shop and he happened to have a '92 Honda Passport SUV that he was willing to sell me for a thousand dollars, and he let me make payments. I immediately went down to the Department of Motor Vehicles, took the written driving test, passed it, and scheduled the road test. There was a two-week wait to take the road test, which gave me plenty of time to pay for the Passport and make enough money to pay all the license fees.

On the morning of the driving test, Mom picked me up and we went to Phil's to pick up the car. As luck would have it, the Passport was gone. Phil's partner had given it to somebody as a loaner car. I went into an immediate panic and Phil offered to let me use a little Honda Accord that he had; I couldn't take the Accord, however, because of some issue with the paperwork. So I ended up driving Mom's '99 Tahoe. I knew parallel parking was going to be a pain in that huge truck, 'cause I had never driven it before. So the only practice I got was driving the seven miles from the shop to the Department of Licensing.

Mom had big rims and little tires on that truck, and as if I wasn't nervous enough already, she told me to make sure I didn't scrape her wheels on the curb. I took the test and passed, only getting docked for making one extra forward and back move while parallel parking. We went back to Phil's and by that time the Passport had been returned I drove my new truck to my new little home and showed it to my landlords. I had been out over a month and aside from a few small problems, I felt like I was progressing well.

Everything was going great until the week before my birthday. I was called into my boss's office at the Ramada and was told since the renovation was complete and the hotel was one hundred percent operational again, I was getting laid off. All I could think of was that for some reason I must not have been destined to succeed.

My dad was working as a bartender at a local golf course and I had been in there a few times since my release from prison. I decided to go there to see if I could find anybody that was hiring. Dad said he would look around and check into it for me too.

Cathy had come to my little house to inspect it and be sure that it was suitable for my children to come visit me. After doing so, she agreed that it was in fact suitable. So the next step in my reuniting with my children was to determine a public meeting place at Cathy's discretion. I didn't really care what steps I had to take. I just wanted to see my kids. We agreed to meet in a public park in Renton, southeast of Seattle. The plan was to have a small picnic and toss the football around with the kids.

I hadn't seen them in a very long time so obviously I was nervous. I went down to the park early and waited in anticipation to see the boys. After an hour of waiting, I started thinking, *Here we go again*, but I was not going to leave that park until I saw my kids, no matter what. They arrived an hour and a half late.

For the first few minutes, they were a little apprehensive about me, Charlie more than Josh, because he was so young when Cathy and I were divorced. But after these few relatively uncomfortable minutes, we started throwing the football around. It was a wonderful day and

I felt a bond between my boys and me. I was well on my way to becoming a good father to my children.

I spent the next two weeks petitioning the court to restore some sort of visitation rights. I was awarded every other weekend, every other holiday, and two weeks in the summer. I made forty-two cents an hour while in prison and I had filled out all the paperwork to lower my child support to twenty-five dollars a month per child while incarcerated and that fifty dollars per month was paid every month.

Little did I know that Cathy had gone to court while I was in county jail and was awarded seven hundred forty-two dollars a month per child. So, needless to say, I went forty-one *thousand* dollars in debt while incarcerated. After getting the visitation all straightened out, I began the process of trying to get that huge debt reduced or erased. I went to court and explained to the judge that I had been in prison and made next to nothing during that time, and was only asking for some relief. His response was that the only way I was going to get that debt erased was if Cathy agreed to let go and sign an affidavit that she was relieving me of the debt.

She flat out refused, even though I tried explaining to her that she got practically everything I made while incarcerated, and it didn't seem fair that in the process of trying to be a good person and getting on track after my prison sentence, life was tough enough without having that monster debt looming over my head.

The following week, one of my dad's friends from the club, who owned the machine shop, offered me a job. It was an entry-level machinist job, but I took it immediately. The pay wasn't very good but I was happy for two reasons: first, this could lead to a good career; and second, it provided structure and stability for my continued efforts to stay on the right side of the law. I was well on my way to becoming a productive member of society, and I felt very good about it.

For the next two months, I put my nose to the grindstone working four 10-hour shifts, and spending my weekends either with my kids or hanging out with my dad at the golf course, playing golf or sitting at the bar drinking beer and watching sports.

Prison wasn't too far in my past, and I still had a little bit of what they called prison mentality—things like always watching my back, being aware of my surroundings and, no matter what, always prepared to defend myself at any given moment. I was sitting at the bar enjoying a beer and a man I had met maybe once or twice before came up to me. His name was Walt. He asked me if we could talk outside. My first thought was that this guy had a beef with me so I walked outside preparing for a fight. To my surprise, as soon as he walked outside he turned around and gave me a big hug, and said, "Johnny you have no idea how much respect people have for you up here."

"Why?" I asked.

"You have defeated what they say can't be beat, methamphetamine addiction!"

I became very emotional; the floodgates opened and the tears were flowing freely as I said "Thanks."

At that moment, Walt and I became good friends. I spent a lot more time up at the bar now because I finally felt like I was part of something. Everybody there was very fond of my dad so therefore they liked me. I worked the second shift so I got to spend a lot of time on the golf course. I actually got to the point where I was consistently hitting the ball relatively well and really enjoying the game. My boys were spending every other weekend with me and I had a good job in a machine shop. Everything was really starting to fall into place and my life seemed to be on the right track. Cathy and I were even getting along.

Even though I had a very fragile sense of security which I was tightly holding onto, I was starting to feel very confident in my ability and my training was going very well in the machine industry. I was putting out very good work at a very high percentage which led me to believe things were going very well at work. Wrong! I went to my second shift lead man and told him I was ready to start learning how to program the machines rather than just set them and watch them run.

"You won't be going any further with this company for at least five more years," he said.

"I'm a fast learner. I know I could do this well and handle the extra responsibility," I replied.

This pissed him off and he proceeded to make my life miserable. I was taken off the machine that I had become very good at running, handed a broom, and told just to sweep the floors all night. This was not acceptable to me, so I walked off the job. I got a phone call from the day shift lead the following morning and he asked me what the problem was.

"I'll come down so we can meet face-to-face," I said.

He and I met for well over an hour and he told me I could go on day shift and work hand-in-hand with the most experienced people in the company, but I had this deep-seated thought that I would be stepping on other people's toes that were on night shift waiting to go days. It would be unfair to them if I were to leapfrog into a premium job.

"I don't want anybody resenting me for doing that," I said, so I turned him down.

I went job hunting again the next day. I went back to the club and asked my dad if he knew of anybody else hiring because I had quit the job at the machine shop. I explained to him what had happened. He wasn't very happy but he understood where I was coming from.

A few days later I had an interview with a construction company that specialized in concrete construction. I got the job and started work the next day, back in the training regiment. This was very hard work and I was twice the age of just about everybody on the crew, but I held my own without much of a problem. After all my time in prison climbing mountains with trees and digging trails around forest fires, I was in pretty damn good shape. I worked hard and learned as much as I could about concrete, building forms, playing Rebar, pouring and finishing. The weekends I didn't have my boys were usually spent on the golf course, in the bar, or doing small odd jobs for friends of the family. I bought myself a Cadillac Seville and once again things seemed to be going very well.

One weekend I went to Enumclaw to get my kids, and to swing by Dale and Brenda's house. When I got down there, Dale and I spent about an hour and a half talking about memories from long ago while the kids played football on an empty lot right around the corner. We decided to go get pizza so Dale and I headed down to the pizza place. My Cadillac was fast and a Corvette pulled up next to me, revving his engine, and Dale said, "I don't think you can take him."

That was all I needed to hear. Testosterone took over and the race was on. He had me by about two car lengths off the line but I quickly passed him and won the race. This was a great moment all the way until the engine started knocking. Shit! I blew the engine, and I knew it.

We called Dale's brother, who had a car trailer, and asked him to come tow my car to my mechanic. Yet another stupid decision on my part. Thirty-five hundred dollars later the Cadillac was fixed so I drove it right across the street and traded it in on a trailblazer.

With the back child support looming over me I thought there was no way I would get a loan, but because I didn't have any negative credit for the past five years, they financed me. It was back to work the next Monday morning so I really focused on keeping my nose to the grindstone because now I had a car payment to worry about. Over the next few months, I worked, played golf, and did odd jobs on the side.

I was on my way home from work one day in the trailblazer and I made an illegal right turn getting onto the freeway. A state patrol officer saw me make that turn and I spotted him right away. I knew I was getting pulled over so I took the next exit and pulled off to the side. He came up to my car and explained to me that he witnessed me making this illegal turn. He asked me to give him my license and registration and then proceeded to ask me to step out of the car, which I did. He searched me, handcuffed me, and put me in the back of the police car. He then sat in the front seat and asked me when was the last time I used drugs. By this time, two other police cars had shown up. I told him I hadn't used in eight years. He then asked me if there were any drugs in the vehicle. Now I was getting a little bit angry. In a smart-ass tone, I told him no, and to feel free to search the vehicle.

Then I added, "Take a vacuum, though, because the truck needs to be cleaned anyway." Yet another example of my alligator mouth overloading my canary ass.

In other words, my mouth got me in trouble again. He spent about thirty minutes digging through my truck, then came back, got me out of the police car, uncuffed me, and told me I was free to go. But he did hand me a ticket for making an illegal right turn.

I then said laughingly, "And you're still giving me a ticket after that bullshit?"

"Just get in your car and go and quit being a smart ass or I'm gonna arrest you."

I called my dad and told him what had happened and that I felt it was blatant harassment because of my prior conviction and record. He told me to calm down and reminded me that for the first five years after prison I would have to put up with this kind of crap, and to just let it go. So I did.

I got tired of the trailblazer after about eight months so I went down to the dealer and bought myself a 2002 Chevy Avalanche. I loved that truck and the kids loved it too. They said it was a great tailgating truck. I was keeping in close contact with Dale and Brenda. Dale had mentioned to me that his brother John lived in the Everett area and that I should get in touch with him. I called John to say Hi. We had partied some prior to my going to prison.

We got together the following weekend and did a lot of drinking. John had gotten off drugs also and was still working at the local airplane manufacturer. We started spending a lot of time together which meant we did a lot of drinking together. John had started dating a girl named Noreen, and one night the two of them went out to continue drinking after we went to dinner. I didn't go with them because I decided to go to work early the next morning. I had two beers at dinner, had another beer, and then went home to bed. I got a tearful phone call at eleven-thirty from Noreen. John had just been arrested for his third DUI. She asked me to come down to the Everett substation and pick them up. So I got dressed and went to the station where I introduced myself to the police officer and let him know who I was there for. He asked me if I had been drinking that night and I told him yes, I had had two beers with dinner and one beer after dinner, then went to bed, and I had been sleeping for well over three hours.

He did a quick field sobriety test with me, which I thought was ridiculous because I was nowhere near the illegal limit. He told me to drive safe and released John to me. I got John in the truck and headed out of the parking lot. The police officer followed me out and as soon as I hit the city street he hit his lights and pulled me over; no questions asked, just arrested me for driving under the influence.

He took me back to the Everett substation and had me blow into the breathalyzer. I blew a .089 and found out later that when I went to sleep my metabolism slowed way down and did not absorb the alcohol as fast, so the police officer knew I was over the legal limit yet he still released John to me. This was full-blown entrapment.

I went to court and with my prior felony convictions the judge made it very apparent that she was going to make an example of me and punish me to the fullest extent of the law. This was another example of double jeopardy, in my opinion. The DUI ended up costing me well over fifteen thousand dollars, my license was suspended seven times, I was arrested twice and spent ten days in jail, had an interlock device in my vehicle for well over two years, and was on probation for three years. This was approximately five times the penalty that her first offense DUI carried.

When I reported to my probation officer, I recognized her from a pawn exchange a month prior to that. She was in there selling jewelry and once again, letting my alligator mouth overload my canary ass, I informed her that I saw her pawning jewelry. She denied it emphatically. My mouth got me into more trouble. She requested that the judge put me on an additional year of probation. Finally the judge said no she had had enough. I did all my time and told my probation officer to back off; this was after the exceptional sentence that I had already served.

Through the years, I had stayed in contact with Sammy, the hair salon owner mentioned earlier, and he introduced me to a guy who had just graduated from USC and was breaking into the movie industry as a director. He and I talked at length and I was asked if I would do the construction for a major motion picture he was working on. There were a couple of very prominent stars in the film and Norm was very good at what he did, so I was really impressed. I worked on the set for six weeks, building, watching the filming, and hanging out with the stars and Norm.

The red carpet was rolled out at the film's première and I took my mom, Josh and Charlie with me. I liked the movie but Mom and the boys didn't. In fact, when the movie was over, Charlie said, "Dad, that was really cool seeing your name in the credits, but please don't ever make us sit through that movie again."

I continued working for the construction company and was doing quite well with the work. Two weeks later, I went home to my little house in Lynnwood, parked my Avalanche in the driveway and went to bed. I woke up at five a.m., looked outside, and the Avalanche was gone! Somebody had stolen my truck. I immediately called the Lynnwood Police Department and reported my truck stolen. They took my name, driver's license number and address. Ten minutes later they called back to tell me they were going to send an officer over because they believed that I paid somebody to steal my truck. Obviously, because of my prison record, they didn't believe me, and were not going to put an ounce of effort forth to help out a criminal.

The truck was found in downtown Seattle rolled over and totaled. The police were adamant that I paid somebody to steal my truck. I was furious. I contacted the insurance company and they put a special investigator on it. Four months later, she approved my claim and they offered me three thousand dollars for the truck. This was absolutely preposterous! This was a fourteen thousand dollar truck and the insurance company was only offering me three grand. Wow, really? So I fought this for well over a month to no avail and finally got so angry that I called the insurance commissioner, explained my situation, and three days later they cut me a check for nine thousand dollars, which barely paid for the truck.

On November 29, 2009, we were setting up for a wall pour. I was setting vertical plywood forms with my lead man who was standing on scaffolding. I was on a footing and handed him up a four-by-eight foot piece of plywood. When he grabbed it from me he pulled it up over the edge of the scaffolding and the bottom of it kicked out, hit me in the chest, and knocked me over backwards. I fell approximately eleven feet into an elevator shaft that had a poured pad on the bottom with Rebar sticking up in multiple places.

God was looking out for me again because I landed flat on my back, basically with Rebar everywhere around me. Amazingly, I didn't get impaled. I turned my left foot almost a hundred eighty degrees, however, and blew out my knee. I got up, hobbled out of the hole, and headed up for the job shack. I was in excruciating pain and couldn't put any weight on that leg. I got to the job shack and told Joe, the superintendent, what had happened and that my knee was very, very sore. He told me if I filed an L and I claim I would be fired immediately upon returning to work.

"That's illegal," I told him. "This is a legitimate claim."

He just laughed. "We'll figure out a way to get rid of you."

It was my grandmother's birthday and we were all going out to dinner that night. As soon as I got to Grandma's house, my grandpa, dad, and my mom took one look at my knee and said I needed to have it looked at. Mom called one of her friends who was an orthopedic surgeon and asked her if I could come in and see her. She agreed.

The following morning I went to her office and when she took one look at my knee she said I needed an MRI. So I asked her if I could just pay for the MRI and if it turned out that it was a serious injury I would fill out the L and I paperwork and file a claim. She then informed me that an MRI cost eighteen hundred dollars. I didn't have that kind of money so I filled out the paperwork.

The MRI showed a torn MCL, and she referred me to a knee specialist. I hobbled into his office, he did a full exam on the knee, took a look at the MRI, and opted for me to go to physical therapy, because he felt the tear would mend itself. I went to physical therapy for four months and the knee not only was not getting better; it was getting worse. I went back to the doctor and told him about the pain I was feeling in the knee and he decided that he wanted to go in and do arthroscopic surgery to try to mend it or at least get a closer look inside. So I went in for surgery on April 15, 2010.

After the surgery the doctor informed me that the MCL had so much scar tissue it probably wasn't going to get any better and that he had found multiple contusions on my meniscus. He scraped away nearly one third of it. I went back to physical therapy for three more months and proceeded to get retrained in a job that would accommodate my ruined knee. I went through all the assessments intelligence testing and the State's rehabilitation service placed me at a community college to retrain me in a clerical capacity. I was not about to be confined to a desk for the rest of my life so I did everything I could to change their minds and let me get into something in the construction industry that would keep me out on a jobsite, not behind a desk.

So Crissy, the counselor from L and I, signed me up for a couple of business management classes and architectural blueprint reading. I liked those classes, but I had a lot of trouble in Typing Skills 101 and Computer Programming 101. I was not cut out to do anything relating to paperwork or computers. So I opted out.

Getting Washington State Labor and Industries to release me and allow me to get a job and get off of the State's nipple was next to impossible. It took two years to finally get off L and I. I was told I had nine percent disability in my left leg and I would be receiving a ten thousand dollar check from the State for a settlement. Two weeks later, I got an envelope from the state. Excitedly, I opened it up and it was a bill for thirty-one hundred dollars! Are you kidding me? This was absolutely ridiculous!

Once again, bad things just happened to follow me wherever I went. Mom and Dad would always say that I had a black cloud that always hung over me.

Meanwhile, my grandpa Doug, who was my mentor and possibly my best friend, had full-blown emphysema and was on twenty-four hour oxygen. I spent a lot of time at Grandma and Grandpa's house hanging out with them, on the average three to four days a week.

Grandpa and I would exchange Navy stories and just hang out talking about hunting trips and working on houses. I made it a point that every time I did a job I would make sure to call Grandpa and ask him questions whether I knew the answer or not. I felt it always made him feel useful and needed, because the emphysema had made him so short of breath that he couldn't take five steps without catching his breath.

One day I got a phone call from Grandpa saying that there was a bad odor in the house. I went over and we figured out that it was a broken sewer pipe somewhere under the house. He called the plumbing company to come out and give him a bid. They did and told him that his driveway had to be ripped up and they would have to replace a large section of sewer pipe. Their bid was over fifteen thousand dollars. I looked at the situation under the house and came to the conclusion that there was only a small section that needed to be taken out. So one of Grandpa's friends and I brought the jackhammers and busted out a four-by-four foot section of concrete and prepped everything for the plumbing company to come out and fix the pipe. This saved well over eleven thousand dollars for Grandpa.

The pipe was fixed and secured and Grandpa and I talked about doing some sort of concrete design outside the back door. Because of all our past elk hunting trips we decided to do an elk design. I rented the concrete stamp of an elk and poured the concrete, broom finished it and then stamped the elk into it. I let it cure for a week and then bought different colors of paint so I could paint a tree backdrop, colored in the antlers, and painted a little lake behind the elk. It turned out really nice and Grandpa was very happy. Grandpa and I remained very close for the rest of his life.

On Mother's Day 2011 my mom decided to take Grandma out shopping and to a movie, and because of Grandpa's failing health she asked if I would stay with him for the day, which I was happy to do. He didn't look very good and he was having more difficulty than usual breathing. Grandpa was a man amongst men and would never admit weakness, so when I asked him how he was feeling, he replied that he was just having a rough day and not to worry.

I spent a wonderful day with Grandpa. Mom and Grandma got home and we sat around for twenty or thirty minutes, then Mom and I headed for Mukilteo. Less than three hours later, the phone rang and it was Grandma saying that Grandpa couldn't catch his breath and that his oxygen wasn't working right. At a sprint I headed out to my truck and Mom followed me, suggesting that my brother, who lived a lot closer, go take care of the oxygen machine. So Trevor went over and I walked him through how to clean the filters and get his oxygen back up to a reasonable range, which he did. I asked Grandpa how he was feeling and he thanked me. Trevor then headed back home.

An hour and a half later Grandma and Grandpa's next-door neighbor called, saying that Grandma was in the driveway screaming that Grandpa was again having a hard time breathing. They had already called the aid car and Mom and I jumped in my truck and headed down there at breakneck speed. The whole time Mom was saying over and over again that Grandpa couldn't die. I couldn't imagine being without my grandfather, my best friend, my mentor.

When Mom and I arrived the paramedics were already there working on Grandpa. We waited in the living room and I heard the paramedics asked for epinephrine three times. the whole time trying to keep my grandfather alive. After three shots of epinephrine straight to the heart, I knew in my heart it was over but wasn't willing to accept it. Mom had a hard time accepting it also. They lost him on the way to the hospital and the whole family met down there.

This was quite possibly the hardest thing I had ever experienced. I couldn't believe Grandpa was gone. I spent the next couple of days helping out around the house and trying to figure out how to do the unthinkable, tell my kids! I decided it was best that I go down to their house, sit them down and tell them that he was in a better place now. They knew something was wrong just by looking at my face. The first thing I said to them was that Grandpa loved them dearly. Both Josh and Charlie knew exactly what was next, and the floodgates opened. Fighting back the tears, trying to be strong for my kids, I told them Grandpa was in a better place, probably mowing God's lawn or working on his car. We had a long discussion, with a lot of tears, a few laughs, and a ton of great memories that we talked about. Everybody who ever knew Grandpa loved him dearly.

Over the next three weeks, my aunt, who lived in Florida, decided that because of my past I should not be allowed to visit Grandma. This was a crushing blow to me, especially after visiting them three or four times a week over the past four years. But she was convinced that I was a bad person and that I was out to steal from Grandma or hurt her. I had no idea how to deal with this new problem. I was speechless. She went so far as to tell the attorney for my grandparents that I was bad news, so the attorney informed both Grandma and my mom that it was best that I stay away.

Reluctantly, I did exactly that, for fear that if I was to go over there, my aunt would file some sort of a restraining order or elder abuse order, or something that would get me back in trouble with the law. It was difficult not to see Grandma the three or four times a week that I was used to.

I spent the next year to year and a half doing nothing but side jobs, and as time went on I earned a relatively good reputation with my construction abilities. I was spending a lot of time with my kids and working hard at building a business. During this time I spent an awful lot of time running around trying to pick up extra work so I could make ends meet. This had proven to be relatively difficult because I only averaged about three hours of sleep a night. This insomnia had been going on for well over twenty years, but you never get used to it. But I remained focused on my sobriety and drug-free life.

At times, functioning with so little sleep proved to be detrimental to my outlook on life. Sometimes I would toss and turn until five or six in the morning, which made it difficult to maintain a positive outlook and a good attitude when I was meeting prospective clients. Thankfully, my mom and dad had a very large circle of friends who always needed small jobs done around their houses. So I was keeping my head above water, barely!

As Mom and Dad's fiftieth anniversary was approaching, my friend John and I decided to pour a custom-stamped kidney-shaped patio in the backyard of their Mukilteo home, along with two waterfalls and a forty-foot streamed that all dropped into a Koi pond. We poured the patio and stamped a river rock pattern into it. Once it was all finished we filled it up with water. It was gorgeous. I was so proud of that custom yard.

Mom and Dad were very happy with the way it turned out. I found that I really loved this type of work. It was very labor-intensive but the reward was amazing, and allowing the creativity to flow was a wonderful feeling and very therapeutic for me. Mom and Dad had a patio party to show off my work, and it was a huge success. For the next year and a half we really enjoyed the backyard at that house.

Soon after finishing the patio, I had decided to join an online dating site. This wasn't too bad except for the fact that I had no idea how to introduce myself to women. Should I tell them about my past or should I hide it? Hmm…well, I decided that honesty was the best policy. And for that reason this wasn't too easy, because I realized that people were very judgmental about my being an ex-con.

I did meet a lady named Heather and after quite a few weeks of emailing and phone conversations we decided to go out. She lived on Camano Island, a little over an hour's drive from my home. I drove up to Camano to meet her and she never showed up. I was just shattered; all I could think of was *who would do this?* This was so cruel, or so I thought. I called her a few times and got no answer. On the one hand I was pissed, but for the most part I was worried that something bad had happened to her. This was just my luck; nothing ever went my way. I could not believe it. But I tried to keep a positive attitude and give her the benefit of the doubt.

I finally got ahold of her the following day. We made arrangements to meet at a casino. I guess I was a glutton for punishment because I agreed to drive all the way up to Marysville, again about an hour's drive, to meet her the following weekend. I found myself having butterflies because this was the first real date that I was going to go on since my release from prison. I got there half an hour early, and she showed up twenty minutes late; I guess that would be fashionably late.

At that point I kind of figured that she wasn't going to show up again so I was extremely excited when she did. We went into the casino and played a couple of slots and then had dinner and ended up at the mall, shopping. I really enjoyed that evening with Heather and I think she did too. We sort of began dating, even though we didn't live that close to each other. She would spend a couple of days at a time in Lynnwood with me when we got together. Over the course of the next two months, we only got together about twice a month.

One day she called and told me that she needed to talk to me and she was heading down to my house. My first thought was that she was pregnant. That's all I needed! I was wrong. When she got there she informed me that she was a methamphetamine addict, and she believed that God had put me in her life to help her get off the drugs. So I told her I'd be there for her when she decided to quit. We remained friends but stopped dating. She did get clean a few months later.

Although I had enjoyed being with Heather, meeting women wasn't a top priority for me. Finding work was more important. I picked up a job in the Renton area building a fence and an electric gate, and the job entailed pouring an entire strip of concrete all the way across the backyard, setting footings, and doing a custom lattice on top. The fence was eight feet tall. As I was doing all my prep work, setting my post, and drawing out the gate design, I was walking around to the side of the house and suddenly spotted a red motorcycle underneath a cover. I peeked under the cover and found it was a Honda crotch rocket! Immediately my wheels started turning in my head. I wanted that bike! So I negotiated with the homeowner to take the motorcycle as a partial trade for the fence.

Over the course of the next two weeks, we went through multiple design changes because the gate, being fifteen feet long and eight feet tall, was way too heavy to be suspended without massive supports. I loaded the motorcycle in the back of my truck and took it home. It hadn't been run in a few years so it required some minor repairs and a tune up, and I was ecstatic because I finally had a motorcycle again and it didn't cost me any out-of-pocket funds. I began riding it every chance I got.

One day I was heading to my parents' house, and was about three miles from my place, rounding a corner. To my surprise, a little Acura rounded the corner at a high rate of speed and began drifting towards me sideways. I had to make a quick decision! Get hit by the oncoming car head-on, or hit the curb. I was doing about thirty-five. I chose the curb, hit it, and went down. The car sped off rapidly.

The driver of a car who was behind the Acura pulled over to render assistance to me. He asked me if I was okay. I couldn't pick the bike up off the ground. For some reason, I didn't have any strength. Totally frustrated, I asked him, "Could you help me pick this goddamned motorcycle up?"

He helped me pick it up, I got back up on it, started it, said thanks, and rode my wrecked motorcycle home. The fairing was broken, the side was all scratched up, handlebars bent and the mirrors missing. I got it up the driveway, parked it and went inside. I was having some difficulty breathing so I lay down thinking I had a pinched nerve in my back or something. About ten minutes went by and my breathing became more labored. I figured it might be time to call 911, so I did, reluctantly.

Living off the beaten path up a winding driveway and beginning to get really worried because I was having a hell of a time breathing, I figured I should walk down to the bottom of the driveway to meet the ambulance. So I forced myself off the bed, but unable to catch my breath, I sat back down again. I sat there for a minute or two then I struggled to get up. I walked down the driveway and got to the bottom just about the same time the ambulance pulled up. The paramedic got out, took one look at me and asked, "What the hell is wrong with you?" He immediately hooked me up to oxygen and had me lying in the back of the ambulance.

We got to Stevens Hospital, they cut my shirt off and told me that I had a broken clavicle and a punctured lung. I spent four days at Harborview after they transported me from Stevens. The motorcycle sat in the driveway, wrecked and undriveable, for the next few months. On Christmas Day, there was a huge windstorm and a two hundred-foot fir tree came down and crushed the motorcycle. Even though it wasn't rideable, I was devastated.

I picked up a few new clients in the Edmonds area and started expanding my scope of work. In August 2011 I applied for a job at a sheet-metal manufacturing company in Woodinville and was hired right away, which was surprising with my criminal background. Once I got the job and started working, the stress of making ends meet was not quite as intense as it had been due to the fact that I was making a regular paycheck now. I started out as a machinist, but the milling machine they had was a single axis with an antiquated computer programming setup. This made it kind of difficult because I was used to running a multiple axis machine at the prior machine shop. The person training me was very territorial, but all in all a really nice guy. He had his own method of doing things and he appeared to be very secretive about some aspects of the job.

After a few weeks I was sent to another part of the shop to learn how to operate the big sanders and deburring equipment. Six months after starting this job, I was asked if I wanted to work three twelve-hour days, which was perfect for my situation. I would have four days a week to work on home remodel and repair jobs. This would be very detrimental to my time spent with my kids, though. I contacted Cathy and told her about the offer and the shift change. She was very understanding and agreed to let me have the kids whenever they were out of school, on spring break, winter break, midwinter break, and pretty much whenever I wanted the kids during the summer.

Once again my life seemed to be falling into place. Once the pressure was lessened, I began researching the VA to begin focusing on trying to get some help for the PTSD I suffered from, or at least thought I suffered from. After hundreds of phone calls and multiple visits to different factions of the military, I was having no luck, mostly because my discharge was Other than Honorable.

I went to a psychologist and had a five-hour visit. The doctor's assessment was that I definitely had PTSD and ADHD. He told me I was extremely intelligent, which evidently was a very bad combination, coupled with ADHD and compounded by PTSD. I took that diagnosis to the military Purple Heart Association, along with my hearing test from my employer, which proved that not only was I suffering from PTSD but I also had a seventy percent hearing loss in my left ear from working on the flight deck.

The representative at the Purple Heart read my file and told me that I definitely was a candidate for some sort of compensation.

All I could think of was the two hundred fifty-two people who died on October 23, 1983 in Beirut, Lebanon.

I was denied, so I reapplied and was denied again. This went on for well over a year. Phone call after phone call, meeting after meeting, and multiple phone conversations with the VA and the American Legion, all to no avail. In February 2012, I was coming up on five years out of prison and started focusing on getting my criminal record expunged. I contacted a few different attorneys and law firms to see what I had to do to start the process of getting myself a clean slate and a fresh start. What I found out was that it was a very long and expensive process and not very easy to accomplish.

The thing that bothered me the most was not the fact that I had a criminal record, but the fact that even though I was an American citizen who served my country diligently and was extremely proud to be an American with respect to all who serve to protect the freedom that a lot of people take for granted, I was not allowed to vote! I could understand not having the right to bear firearms, but not being allowed to vote really made me feel like a second-class citizen.

But no matter what hurdles were placed in my path I remained determined to stay positive and always move forward. Life was actually moving forward steadily and I was pretty content. I had a roof over my head, a job, and most important, a great and loving family.

My mom and her best friend, Patsy, had an estate sale business for the past thirty years, so I was getting a lot of small jobs through their company, mostly cleaning out after the sale or moving stuff for people who purchased large items. In September 2012, Mom was doing a sale in Lake Forest Park. The house was beautiful and overlooked Lake Washington. My dad fell in love with it. It was built in the early Fifties and had never been updated so Dad and I sat down and talked. He wanted that house. He asked if I would give him some help in updating and remodeling if he decided to purchase it. All I could think of was all the fun I had following him around when I was a little guy. I took this as a great opportunity to get close to my dad again. So I agreed to help and it was exciting to think about how much fun this project was going to be.

They purchased the house two weeks later and Dad and I immediately started planning the remodel. My job was going well, I had a few decent side jobs, my relationship with my kids was great, everything was going along well. Too well! Something had to go wrong, judging from everything in my past. Dad and I began meeting at the house in Lake Forest Park a couple of times a week, because he wanted to be moved in by Christmas.

I was on my way home from work on a Saturday night around nine-thirty, heading north on I-405 towards my house in Lynnwood. The engine in my truck made a loud bang and the motor locked up, causing the transmission to lock up. The truck went into a slide at sixty miles an hour. I pushed the clutch in to release the tires and coasted to a stop on the side of the highway. When I got the truck pulled over, I could only think I had surely cheated death once again. It took about ten minutes for me to catch my breath and relax. I thought for sure the truck was going to roll over.

I called my parents and let them know what had happened, and got permission from my brother to borrow his extra vehicle until I could figure out what I was going to do. This was definitely the last thing I needed to happen at this point in time, I couldn't afford a new vehicle and I sure couldn't afford a car payment. I went into a pretty severe depression for days. All I kept asking myself was "why me?"

I began shopping for a vehicle, keeping in mind that I needed a truck with an extended cab and a backseat, or an SUV. I found a '94 Chevy full-size pickup with an extended cab and a full-size bed. Some-how, some way they agreed to finance me, so I bought it. The following week it was time to move Mom and Dad into the new house, so the truck came in handy; we had the move finished in three days.

I had built the pond at the other house and Mom had her pet fish that she was worried about, so I had another project to complete ASAP! I could not allow my mom to go through separation anxiety with her fish. *They're fish, for god's sake!* But Mom loves her fish! So the following night I headed to Mom and Dad's new home, shovel in hand, and started digging. It took me nine hours total, but I had a twelve-by-nine foot hole, three feet deep at one end, and four feet deep at the other.

The following afternoon, Dad and I headed down to the fish store. We got the pump, skimmer, liner, underlayment and filtering system. I installed the underlayment and the liner that night. The next day,

I dug a spot for the skimmer box, assembled the waterfall, and installed the filter. That was enough work for the day.

I woke up the next morning and headed down to Mom and Dad's, filled the pond halfway with water, and turned the pump on. Everything worked perfectly so I shut the pump down and started filling the pond the rest of the way. Once I had filled it, I began to get creative with the rock placement. I spent well over six hours moving, setting and placing rocks—big rocks!

Once I got the whole border set the way I wanted it, it was time to cap the waterfall and make sure the skimmer was as covered as possible. This took another two to three hours. Everything looked great. We had to treat the water and let it filter for two days before bringing the fish down. When that was finished, Dad and I went to the Mukilteo house to retrieve the fish. Mom had planned to go with us but we told her she couldn't go because she was too freaked out about her pet fish. I'm sure Mom paced the floor the whole time we were gone. We got the fish in a bucket and transported them to their new home; everything went off without a hitch. It took another couple of weeks to get the surrounding areas finished with pots, pots, and more pots, full of pretty flowers. When they moved in, the upstairs was ninety percent finished and very livable, and Mom had her fish.

My machinist job was going well and getting my parents moved into the new house was a huge load off my shoulders. They found renters for the Mukilteo house, got them moved in and happy, and Mom and Dad were happy, too. My landlord at the Lynnwood house hadn't seen too much of me over the past couple of months because I spent most of my time in Lake Forest Park. In late September I came home to find a note on my door for me to call him. I was informed that I had to move because his daughter was going through a divorce and he wanted her to live there.

Wow, every time things started going good and I was getting comfortable with my life, something would happen to throw me into another tailspin. I got on the phone to start looking for places to live, but still the felonies that hung over my head proved to be detrimental to my finding a decent place to live. Phone call after phone call and rejection after rejection, I was ready to give up. But Mom and Dad and I talked and they said I was welcome to stay in their home as long as

I wanted. So I got a storage unit and moved in with my parents in Lake Forest Park.

For the next few months, I worked my three-day workweek and spent the better part of my days off working at my parents and for Ron and Joanne, friends of my parents. I had done a basement remodel for their son the previous summer, a bittersweet experience because he lived across the street from my grandmother. Knowing that I couldn't go there and say Hi to her was depressing and knowing that her health was failing made it even harder. On top of everything else, I really missed Grandpa Doug.

Ron and Joanne, as well as Mike, became my second family. We had a lot of heartfelt talks about my grandparents. My aunt Diane had really driven a wedge into my ability to be a grandson to my grandmother, so I decided, with the help of my parents and friends, to make it a point to go over and visit Grandma at least once a week. It all began in February 2013. At first, it was rather uncomfortable and I was very nervous, but those feelings slowly subsided. After all, I had spent a lot of time as a child camping with Grandma and Grandpa and, of course, there were all the times I spent over there the past few years.

I was also doing a small job for Grandma's neighbor, Sarah, so I made sure that the times I did go over to Grandma's there were witnesses that would attest to the fact that I did nothing wrong while over there. I knew going there could quite possibly put my freedom in jeopardy, but I decided I really needed to go see her, because I knew when she was gone I would regret it if I hadn't made the effort. I've had quite a few very good clients with whom I've built relationships over the last two years. Frank and Val, Linda and Dawson, Dick and Patsy, and Caroline—to name a few. Bath and kitchen remodeling, building offices, painting basements and exteriors, multiple small jobs—I've really enjoyed the variety of work and the ability to forge new friendships. And I really felt good about the relationship that was being rebuilt with Grandma.

So life was rather hectic, but going well. Whenever I had the kids, I made it a point to take them over to see their great-grandma. Josh and Charlie were on midwinter break in late February, so they spent a couple of days with me. It just so happened that that particular week Aunt Diane was visiting from Florida and staying with Grandma.

My mom convinced me that even if she was there that I should definitely still make a point to get the kids over there to visit. I was hesitant to put myself or my kids in that position but the entire family decided that it was best that I put my pride away and get the kids over there. The visit went relatively well. I held my tongue and didn't say or do anything that I would ever regret.

I started getting a little bit nervous because my job was going well; my side jobs were going well; and most important, I was rebuilding my relationship with my grandmother. Something had to go wrong, judging from past experience. I went to a Safeway store to pick up lunchmeat and bread for work. When I left the store with my purchases, I walked out to the parking lot and my truck was surrounded by police cars. My heart sank. All I could think of was *What the hell's going on?*

I walked over and asked the officers, "Can I help you?" They asked if that was my truck and of course I responded "yes, what's the problem?" They told me to get on the ground, proceeded to handcuff me, and put me in the back of one of the police cars. I was told that this was a high drug-trafficking area and they had run my license plates, and seeing that I had prior felony convictions they evidently thought they should search my truck. I was detained for forty-five minutes then released. All I could think of was, "When is this shit gonna end? My God, I've been out for six years!"

Because of my odd work schedule, my workweek being Friday, Saturday and Sunday, twelve hours a day, I was unable to take part in most holidays such as Easter, Mother's Day, Father's Day etc. The kids came over during spring break in late April to spend a few days with me. We did the usual stuff together, visiting friends, playing putt putt golf and just hanging out, relaxing. And, of course, we made it a point to visit Grandma. At ninety, Grandma had become very frail and in early May she became weaker so Mom took her to the hospital and we learned that she had pneumonia. They kept her for a few days on antibiotics. She was sent home even though she seemed to be getting weaker and weaker with every passing day.

On Mother's Day 2013 I was at work and kind of bummed because I wasn't able to spend Mother's Day with the family. But work was important. At eight-thirty that evening, an hour before my shift's end, Dad called to tell me that Grandma had passed.

EPILOGUE

The teenage years are often the most challenging in a person's life, going through puberty, trying to find your identity, and going through the changes from a carefree child to a young adult. In what seems like the blink of an eye, you go from playing a game of tag or hide-and-seek, to deciding what you want as a career.

At the age of twelve or thirteen, you go from grade school to junior high, from being top dog in grade school, to bottom feeder in junior high. You try to adjust to your environment while counselors and teachers start pressuring you to figure out what you're going to do as an adult.

During this entire time you are faced with peer pressure from your classmates, and you seek acceptance in everything you do. During this transformation in your life between the ages of twelve and sixteen, the unwavering pressure is often overwhelming, the decisions you choose to make will possibly pattern your entire future. If you spend too much time studying or going to the library you get labeled a nerd. If you decide to go behind the school and smoke cigarettes or weed you're labeled a troublemaker.

The labels you pick up when you're thirteen or fourteen are labels that you have to live with for the rest of your school career. Every day as a young teenager presents a new challenge, what to do? Who to hang out with?

As a seventh grader you start going to separate classes instead of being in one classroom all day. So, you're always in a hurry to get to your next class for fear of being late and the ninth graders are dumping your books, detaining you, or picking on you; so not only do you have the pressure of getting from class to class, you have the pressure of avoiding the bigger kids for fear of what they would do if they caught you. Needless to say, aside from the standard pressure of going through all your life changes, puberty and so forth, there is the insurmountable worry of who or what is waiting for you around each corner.

As a father of two teenage boys myself, I wouldn't wish upon my worst enemy what my parents went through with me. The hardest part of this whole scenario is to comprehend the fact that my parents did nothing wrong raising me or my brother. Our mother stayed home with us until we were eleven years old. Dad worked his butt off to keep food on the table. As children, my brother and I never wanted for anything. All of our needs were always met. Dad moved the family into the Magnolia house because it looked like a great place to raise kids. After all, there was a soda fountain, a playfield, bowling alley, and a movie theater.

Everything still fell in my lap with each choice I made as I went through those few years of mounting pressure from what seemed like all angles. As a child, it seemed like my relationship with my dad was a roller coaster. He would be happy with me, then I would do something stupid to piss him off. Over and over again, this was the way it went.

From the time I was twelve years old on, I knew I was much smarter than my dad, until I was about thirty; then suddenly he wasn't so dumb after all. Thankfully, through all the crap my parents went through with me, they were still there for me. The love never stopped. It might get strained and tested time and time again, but it never went away (at least in this family I was blessed to be a part of).

And being a father of my own two sons, I feel the only thing I can do is guide them to the best of my ability so they don't go down the path I went down. I explain to them whenever they are with me that I will always be there for them no matter what, and they are going to make their own mistakes. God knows, I made enough of my own, but I can only hope that they learn a little bit from what I've told them about my life.

Contrary to what anybody says, peer pressure is quite possibly the hardest part of growing up. Throughout my fifty years, my parents have gotten so pissed off at me that they wanted to wring my neck or kick me out of the house for a number of reasons, but the one thing that never faltered was the fact that they have loved me unconditionally.

They say love conquers all. I agree wholeheartedly! The church says we get to experience unconditional love when we get to the pearly gates of Heaven. I get the chance to experience this every day, thanks to the parents I have been blessed with!

This book is dedicated to all the parents who hang in there and show unconditional love for their children, no matter what! I don't think I could have gotten through all the bad choices I made without my parents' love.

I can only hope that there are more parents in the world like the parents I was blessed with.